A LEADER'S LEGACY

AHMED AL ZAROONI

PASSIONPRENEUR®
PUBLISHING

A LEADER'S LEGACY

Leaders Who Create Leaders

AHMED AL ZAROONI

PASSIONPRENEUR®
PUBLISHING

A Leader's Legacy
Copyright © 2024 Ahmed Al Zarooni
First published in 2024

Print: 978-1-76124-136-9
E-book: 978-1-76124-138-3
Hardback: 978-1-76124-137-6

All rights reserved. No part of this book may be reproduced, stored in a retrieval system, or transmitted by any means (electronic, mechanical, photocopying, recording, or otherwise) without written permission from the author.

Because of the dynamic nature of the Internet, any web addresses or links contained in this book may have changed since publication and may no longer be valid. The information in this book is based on the author's experiences and opinions. The views expressed in this book are solely those of the author and do not necessarily reflect the views of the publisher; the publisher hereby disclaims any responsibility for them.

The author of this book does not dispense any form of medical, legal, financial, or technical advice either directly or indirectly. The intent of the author is solely to provide information of a general nature to help you in your quest for personal development and growth. In the event you use any of the information in this book, the author and the publisher assume no responsibility for your actions. If any form of expert assistance is required, the services of a competent professional should be sought.

Publishing information
Publishing and design facilitated by Passionpreneur Publishing
A division of Passionpreneur Organization Pty Ltd
ABN: 48640637529

Melbourne, VIC | Australia
www.PassionpreneurPublishing.com

TABLE OF CONTENTS

Dedication And Acknowledgements — vii

Chapter 1: Learning To Lead Oneself –
The Transformation That Comes From Within — 1

Chapter 2: Mastering Leadership – The Qualities
That Make A Successful Leader — 5

PART 1 — LEADING ONESELF

Chapter 3: Leadership Overview –
The Importance Of Leading Oneself — 19

Chapter 4: Becoming Responsible –
Understanding The Need for Self-Evaluation — 29

Chapter 5: Anchors And Ladders –
Your Environment — 39

Chapter 6: Goals And Planning – How To
Select Goals And Create An Action Plan — 55

Chapter 7: Mastering Your Craft – Applicable
Knowledge Is Power — 63

Chapter 8: Time-Check Priorities By
Time-Blocking – Multitasking And Distractions   75

PART 2   LEADING OTHERS

Chapter 9: Culture – Creating Cultures That Vibe   107

Chapter 10: Rings Of Influence –
Your Role As A Leader   129

Chapter 11: Mastering Team Strengths –
You Are Only As Strong As Your Weakest Link   141

Chapter 12: Environment – Motivational
Approaches In An Organization   155

Chapter 13: Enhancing Connections –
Change, Communication, Trust   163

Chapter 14: Planning And Ownership –
Taking Accountability   179

Chapter 15: Leading One's Boss – Quantity
Versus Quality And Managing Upwards   195

Author Bio   205
Notes And References   207

DEDICATION AND ACKNOWLEDGEMENTS

With deep admiration and profound gratitude, I dedicate this book to our nation's remarkable and inspiring leaders who have left a permanent mark upon the world, and to you for deciding to take on this journey of becoming a future leader.

In this journey of life, I find myself blessed to have been born in a land where, from the time of its inception, the seeds of great leadership have been sown in its very foundation and remain an intrinsic part of our very existence. It is a place where the pursuit of leadership excellence and the relentless drive to be the best resonates within the souls of all its inhabitants.

As I reflect upon this heritage, I am humbled to stand in the shadow of giants – those visionary leaders whose ideals have fortified our journey. Their legacy stands tall, an unshakeable pillar of strength, and a testament to the enduring power of purpose.

May their legacy and unwavering commitments guide us towards a brighter future, reminding us of the extraordinary potential that lies within each and every one of us.

CHAPTER 1

LEARNING TO LEAD ONESELF

The Transformation
That Comes From Within

Life has its moments – turning points that change everything. In fact, moments that are the most difficult or painful are the ones that offer the best opportunities to transform. If you take those opportunities, you can find yourself with a renewed sense of self and purpose. You could say that is what happened to me.

A few years ago, I was facing many struggles. My personal issues affected me deeply, and I was facing a constant mental battle that was wearing me down.

Life tested me to the limits, and there were moments when the agony was unbearable. Those moments were key turning points. I recall them clearly, and how I began to unravel and lose myself in the darkness. I knew that I had choices. I could let myself go, or I could accept the reality and move forward.

I chose to move forward.

My workplace was a long drive from home. On the way there, I would listen to podcasts and audiobooks. And it was during these hours on the road that I began to feel calm. I found clarity. I was able to reflect on myself, and what changes I needed to make. After work, on the way back, I would listen to more books and more insights, and I would return home feeling strangely thrilled by all the knowledge that I was gaining. It helped also that I was not alone at home and spent some good-quality time with my son and mother. Also, I had a dear friend who was there for me during those tough times.

Slowly, as I recovered my balance, I began to realize that my experience, combined with the book knowledge that I had gained over the years, had given me a unique perspective on leadership. My knowledge, through constant reading and listening, was becoming part of who I was, and I was beginning to apply this knowledge in the workplace.

The more I applied my new learnings, the more confident I became. I began to absorb more information and jotted down hundreds of notes about ideas and concepts that had created an impact on me. The whole process taught me patience. It taught me how to work out a plan to achieve a goal.

This became my daily routine. I would write down all the wonderful knowledge gleaned from books, and I read over my notes often. This helped me a lot – the more I read, the more I felt a strong sense of purpose.

My goal was to take my knowledge to the world. I began to feel the excitement of sharing my expertise in a book. This reinforced and resonated with the idea that people's needs mattered to me and I had an ability to understand their motivations.

My low moments helped me realize truths about many aspects of life. I am a stronger and more purposeful person today. Also, I am more at peace with myself and have greater patience with others. I feel more confident in leading others and leading myself. I have greater clarity. And all of this has affirmed that I am meant to be a leader.

When I look back, I realize I have had four years of knowledge accumulation from hundreds of leadership and personal development books, research material, peer-reviewed articles, publications, studies, and statistics. Added to that, I have been a senior executive with over twenty years of corporate experience and have led over 3000 employees in various sectors spanning the banking and health insurance industries. I have an MBA from the UK and multiple certifications in leadership from world-class universities such as the University of Oxford and Harvard University. Additionally, I have been a supervisory board member of a fintech company and have served as a board member for various other companies. All this experience and extensive knowledge, along with a strong results-driven mindset, have made me a passionate leader who focuses on team development, growth, and empowerment.

Therefore, this book aims to guide managers, executives, and leaders in the UAE who aspire to become innovative senior leaders and change advocates through practical strategies and actions so they can accelerate and achieve advancement in their career goals and purpose.

In any sphere of life, leading oneself is the starting point. It is only then that we can lead others.

CHAPTER 2

MASTERING LEADERSHIP

The Qualities That Make A Successful Leader

Have you ever been in a room where someone walks in and, bang, all eyes turn to that person? It is as if they are in a spotlight. There is an aura of sheer power and leadership energy that draws people to this individual.

What is it that this powerful, magnetic person projects that enchants everyone and prompts them to gravitate towards him or her? What kind of qualities does this individual possess?

Let's embark on a journey that explores the profound impact of a magnetic leader's aura, and how a leader masters the craft of leadership to create an everlasting legacy for the future.

A PERSONAL ODYSSEY OF LEADERSHIP

Reflecting upon my own experiences, I feel a constant inner high, greater than any other, that only comes from knowing that you have left a positive mark on the lives of those you are in charge of. There is an unshakable feeling of achievement in seeing individuals flourish under your guidance and an immense gratification that instills a deep sense of confidence and pride.

They say there is a psychological comfort in giving without expecting anything in return. I say, 'The intangible amount that we get back in return is much more than what we can ever give.'

By the time you conclude this book, you will have a comprehensive understanding of the facets that define a leader's role beyond their mere positional authority. Let us dismiss the belief that leaders are distant figures, sitting way up high in ivory towers, disconnected from those they lead. Instead, let us delve deeper and uncover the integral role a leader plays in developing an ever-thriving personal and organizational ecosystem.

The true role of a leader is not to be a mere boss; it is to serve with a genuine commitment towards the growth and development of other leaders while at the same time advancing the organization's objectives with excellence.

A LEADER'S INFLUENCE

Contrary to the misconception that leaders are distant figures, their effectiveness is interlinked with their ability to lead and develop other individuals into future leaders, not followers. Hence, a leader's influence is not restricted to their direct reports but extends down through every level within the organization. This kind of leadership indirectly affects the customers of the organization. We cannot dismiss the fact that the voice of the customer is shaped by the staff.

In reality, leaders are entrusted with the responsibility of shaping the future of the people they are in charge of, and the interactions that occur between the organization and its customers. This extends, but is not limited to, overall customer experience and satisfaction. These symbiotic relationships between leadership, team dynamics, and customers underscore the major influence leaders wield over the shaping of the organization's culture and performance.

THE TRANSFORMATIVE POWER OF THE MIND

The Homo sapien's brain, although small in size, equaling only two to three percent of the overall mass of the human body, is a marvelous apparatus that possesses the ability to shape destinies and conquer challenges that may seem impossible and unattainable at times. However, like any instrument, the mind requires meticulous tuning along with dedication and continuous practice from its owner to be able to reach a high level of mastery and unlock its full potential.

> *'I have not failed. I've just found 10,000 ways that won't work.'*
>
> — THOMAS EDISON

Consider the beautiful mind of Thomas Edison. Through sheer determination, a strong mindset, and an eagerness to prevail, he exceeded all expectations with his innovations that transformed the world. His perspective of looking at failures as stepping stones exemplifies his unshakable belief in the capabilities of the human mind. This is a testament to the growth mindset, a cornerstone of all effective leaders.

HOW CAN YOU FOSTER A GROWTH MINDSET AND DO THE SAME FOR YOUR TEAM?

Let's start by embracing challenges and learning from failure. The fact is that we all face some kinds of setbacks or issues that affect our mindset. However, the key is to blaze a trail through any challenges or obstacles. Being persistent and having the ability to maintain an unwavering determination in the face of setbacks. Understanding that every process takes its own time and you will get there in due time. Stick to the course, keep your focus ahead, and take baby steps. As long as you are following your roadmap, it is taking you a step closer to your desired destination.

When you face your challenges with a growth mindset, you also influence those around you. They want to be like you and learn from you. Tracking your own behavior and receiving feedback helps you to understand yourself and be open to change.

Do not underestimate the power of feedback from mentors, peers, and team members. Let's face it – we all have some imperfections, and we are often blind to them. However, being open to constructive criticism provides the fuel for growth through adaptation and innovation. Be authentic and embrace change. Explore new approaches and be willing to challenge the status quo. This will give you the edge to stay ahead of the pack.

CULTURE

All organizations, like nations, have a culture. The fostering of a robust organizational culture requires a well-thought-out and deliberate approach, encompassing an understanding of, first, the type of culture you would want to cultivate. The next step is to incorporate this with your team's needs and objectives.

Maintain clear accountability and transparency, appreciating each team member and offering a commitment to their safety. This means there is zero tolerance for negative and disruptive behaviors.

The glue that binds individuals from diverse backgrounds into a cohesive tribe is the ability to be accepting and respectful of all. Crafting cultures that resonate within an organization is usually achieved through inspiration, mentoring, and motivation, and through the art of empowerment.

Your ability to build bridges among your team members through open communication and transparency builds trust. This then encourages healthy conflicts amongst the team for the betterment of the organization. By addressing challenges head-on and guiding your teams on how to learn from one another's experiences, an environment where each voice is valued and heard will be created.

This essentially becomes your hallmark for cultivating a thriving and harmonious culture that can withstand the test of time.

As a leader, it falls upon your shoulders to stand as a constant guardian against all negativity, ensuring that the cultural setting becomes one of growth and development.

Part of your duty is to lay a foundation for growth through self-discipline, breaking objectives into actionable measures, tracking progress, and celebrating wins. By doing so, you will be transforming your team into a group of self-driven leaders who will ignite the very essence of a culture that believes in achieving collectively and through collaboration, magnifying the overall success of your entire team and organization.

OPTIMIZATION OF MEETINGS

Meetings, and more meetings, are the bane of many organizations. The higher up the corporate ladder you climb, the more you get dragged into meetings. Learning the art of conducting effective meetings through clear agendas, relevant participant engagement, and effective time management is key to keeping everyone alert during meetings. The cost of having a meeting can be offset by the return on investment you get from having the right people there to foster active involvement, which will cultivate an environment that values time and purposeful interaction while eliminating unnecessary gatherings, AKA 'meetings.'

CULTIVATION OF A LEADERSHIP LIFE CYCLE

The evolution of turning followers into future leaders starts by identifying leadership potential by coaching, mentoring, and guiding them through the art of delegation and decision-making. The ultimate aim is the creation of a network of leaders who, in turn, develop other future leaders, creating an ongoing cycle that cultivates growth and positive transformation.

SURROUNDED BY EXCELLENCE

Common to all effective leaders is a continuous quest for new talent with a certain set of skills that are currently lacking and an ability to integrate them into their teams. 'You are only as strong as your weakest link.' This type of pursuit, when targeted through proper analysis of team strengths and then the infusion of the required diverse array of strengths and capabilities, will be your way towards cultivating a culture of excellence.

Harnessing the strengths of your team members will allow you to leverage each individual's potential. By aligning organizational tasks and objectives to the strengths of the individual team members, you will optimize your team's performance. Just as a maestro leads his orchestra to create a classical melody through a collective effort, you too will be able to bring the perfect rhythm of success to your organization.

One of the strongest skills that you can obtain and should aim to be known for as a leader is the creation of strong, solid teams. Once you have achieved that, focus on your direct reports. Give them instructions to create their own solid teams with timelines to deliver. Then give them the space to focus, identify their weakest links, and build their individual teams through fair monitoring and reporting.

TEST THE WATERS

While actively engaging in talent tracking, do not forget the hidden gems that you might have within the organization. Be a leader that schedules time with someone in a more junior role. Embrace skip-level meetings to uncover such gems. Once you see a spark, delegate some work and added responsibilities to see if they are willing to go the extra mile, and if they have the potential to be a future leader who, if nurtured well, would be an asset to the organization.

THE ART OF SELECTION

As I mentioned before, one of your main aims should be to develop solid, strong teams. This is what you want to be known for as a 'leader maker.' Once you have this title under your belt, a world of opportunities will be flung open for you. Choose individuals whose values and goals align with your team's and organization's overarching objectives. By doing so, you will create a body of leaders who strive for excellence.

PLANNING AND EXECUTION

Planning and execution are like two sides of the same coin. For a leader, the coin does not exist if both are not crafted meticulously. Perfect execution of a poor plan will always remain poor, while the best-laid plans with poor execution will most probably never see daylight.

The pillars that hold this bridge that spans across one another's boundaries are constructed upon accountability and ownership, transforming your visionary aspirations into successful and tangible outcomes.

You, as a leader, bear the dual responsibility of not only designing a meticulous plan but also instilling a profound sense of accountability and ownership within your teams. The smart way to perfect execution is through a buy-in process that commences at the initial planning stages with the early involvement of all those who can breathe life into your plan. This comes about by encouraging their active participation at the time of the plan's inception, creating ownership and unity amongst the team members.

GUARDIANS OF RESPONSIBILITY

Leaders are responsible not only for the orchestration of plans and the cultivation of ownership; they shoulder the responsibility for the entire team. Whether triumph has been obtained or relinquished, your team's outcome is the real reflection of your leadership, and it is what you will be judged upon. Leaders do not play the blame game; they wear the cloak of responsibility and acknowledge their pivotal role in steering the course as captain of the ship. When they reach their destination successfully, they share the credit with their team and take the blame upon themselves if they fail.

FAIR BUT FIRM

Your team should be aware that in the pursuit of a culture of excellence, fairness is a key ingredient, and kindness should never be seen as a weakness. It falls upon all members of the team to take ownership of their actions and to be accountable. The application of this principle fosters trust and encourages each team member to deliver their best. When each team member understands what they will be held accountable for and how they will be rewarded, it will create a cycle of excellence where high performers will thrive and inefficiencies will be overshadowed by the collective pursuit of brilliance.

FINAL NOTES

As you dive deeper in your expedition through the realms of leadership within this book, the threads of each lesson learnt will come together to form a wider, more profound insight.

Emerging from each journey, you will stand as an architect, a master craftsman forging your own legacy, and guiding those who are entrusted to your command to reach their full potential and become leaders who create leaders. Your deliberate actions will go beyond the ordinary, ascending towards a realm where mediocrity shall yield to the extraordinary.

The true art of leadership can only be mastered by those who can bring harmony as part of the art of leading oneself, and the art of leading others – by uniting people in the same way that two notes are united to compose an everlasting melody.

PART 1

LEADING ONESELF

A leader is one who faces reality, takes ownership of his actions, identifies weaknesses, and focuses on developing strengths.

PART I

SAVING ONESELF

CHAPTER 3

LEADERSHIP OVERVIEW

The Importance Of Leading Oneself

'The ruler, any ruler, is only there to serve his people and secure for them prosperity and progress. To achieve this, he should live among his people to feel their wishes and know their problems, and this cannot be achieved if he isolates himself from them.'

— HIS HIGHNESS, SHEIKH ZAYED BIN SULTAN AL NAHYAN, FATHER OF OUR NATION, FOUNDER AND FIRST PRESIDENT OF THE UNITED ARAB EMIRATES

In order to lead, guide, and look after others, we must first lead and look after ourselves. Just like when we are traveling on a flight before take-off, the flight attendant reminds us that in the case of an emergency, the oxygen masks will fall. The first priority for us is to put on our own masks, and then attend to others.

This is true in all aspects of life. If we do not look after ourselves first, we will have limited capacity to look after others, and sometimes no capacity at all.

Before we lead others, we must first be clear on our own purpose, vision, and direction. We need to be clear about our own goals. We need to have a pre-set destination in mind and then a plan in place to ensure we are able to reach this destination, along with the resources needed to arrive there.

To illustrate this point, say you are to take a flight from Abu Dhabi to London. The pilot has to be prepared and clear on what he will be doing, and in order to do that, he has to get the information needed to do his job right. He needs to know the plane size, the passenger capacity, the speed at which to travel, the weather conditions, and the location of the departure and arrival landing strips. After that, he will follow the plan and directions at the right altitude to a T. This is done with regular check-ups in order to ensure that all procedures are followed and the plane is on track to reach the destination successfully.

QUALITIES THAT CREATE A LEADER MINDSET

A leader's skillset needs to include the ability to be precise in planning and preparing to lead an organization. There are many moving parts in any organization or workplace project, and these have to be checked and double-checked to ensure that the leader is on track to take their organization on a flight to success. And it needs to be emphasized that a leader's responsibility extends much further beyond the standard definition of 'to lead.'

The word 'leadership' originates from the old English word *laeden*, which means to guide or conduct. The modern English word – leader – has been used since the 14th Century and refers to a person who guides, directs, or commands a group or organization.

Leadership is, therefore, a skill, and like any skill, it can be learned and developed. Every great leader was once a follower, a learner, and evolved to become a person capable of setting an example for others. The fact is that people who become leaders don't necessarily have to be born with leadership skills. They can learn them throughout life; they can develop these skills through personal growth and self-development. Leaders are motivated and eager to learn. They are not afraid of making mistakes because they know mistakes are opportunities to learn more. They have a strong idea of what they want to achieve in life and work hard to master the abilities they need to get there.

A leader shares their vision with passion and enthusiasm, inspiring others to believe in their mission too. It is this kind of magnetic quality that attracts people towards such a person. The future is unknown, and the one who has clarity and confidence in the future that they envision, for the betterment of the organization, is what makes such a person stand out.

A VISIONARY LEADER MINDSET

Imagine that you have a friend called Saif who works in the airport at the ticketing desk. It is Friday morning, and he sees a young lady step into the airport lobby and approach his desk.

'Good morning. My name is Saif. How can I assist you today?'

'Good morning. My name is Lamya, and I want to buy a ticket for the next flight, please,' the lady replies with a beautiful smile.

What do you think Saif's next question is going to be?

'Where to?'

'Anywhere. It does not matter,' says Lamya.

'Miss, I need a destination or I cannot proceed with your request.'

'Oh, yes, you can. Check your system and tell me what the price and destination for the next flight are and book me that ticket.'

'Are you sure you want to go anywhere?' Saif asks with a confused look.

'For the last time, just book the ticket,' says Lamya.

Was Saif right to be confused by Lamya's request and behavior? Did her request confuse you? Saif was more than confused. He thought Lamya was insane!

Did you think the same? Maybe a little bit, or that there was something wrong with her?

You are absolutely right.

We all know that traveling requires thought. Going on a vacation needs planning. We first plan which city we want to go to, say London. We begin exploring all angles.

Research: How do we get the visa? How do we apply for the visa? What's the weather like in London?

Work: Do we have annual leave or not? For how many days do we take leave?

Budget: How much will it cost? Are we going to travel business, first, or economy class? To Heathrow or Gatwick Airport? Where will we be staying? Where will we be dining?

Transport: How will we be moving around the city? Cab, train, bus, or rented car?

So much thought goes into a vacation, a journey, a destination. So much thought about a place we will only be going to for a couple of days or weeks.

Yet, if someone asks us, **'Where will you be five years from now and how will you get there?'**

WE HAVE NO ANSWER, NO PLAN, NO IDEA.

Why? Because it is convenient to say that we don't know what the future holds, so why create a definite plan? The fact is that you can have dreams and goals, a big vision or an idea that can create change. You do have the capacity and the ability to create a future for yourself, and for others, that is positive and filled with success.

If we thought Lamya was insane for not having a plan or destination in mind for traveling, what are we for not having a plan and destination for our own lives?

Whether we like it or not, we are all one of the passengers in this journey called life. If we do not have a destination in mind, we will still be going somewhere. The only difference is that, as with drifters, it will not be the destination of our choice. We might reach the North Pole, in khaki shorts, looking out of place, only to be discovered, chased, and maybe even eaten by a polar bear!

BEGIN WITH YOURSELF

Leading yourself first is the start of your journey to leadership. Before you start to lead or direct anyone, you need to make sure your vision for yourself is clear and that your destination is defined. A leader does not drift aimlessly through life, ignorant of where they are going, or what is waiting for them when they get there. The story of Saif and Lamya demonstrates this perfectly.

Having a vision, a plan, and a destination is vital in all aspects of life. Neglecting our plan for the future leads to a future of chance, where you might one day reach London but, then again, you may end up at the North Pole as dinner for a hungry polar bear!

Reflect on your purpose and vision that you want to reach. And then research, plan, and ask yourself if you have what it takes to get there. Take some time to reflect on this.

Become the pilot of your own life. Set a destination, guide your aircraft with meticulous precision, and reach your destination with a flawless landing. Leadership cannot be inherited. It is a skill, and like all skills, it can be learnt and developed through patience and the right plan for personal growth and development.

ACTIONS FOR YOU

Define your vision: Write down what your burning desire is, where you want to be, and what you want to be known for. How will this vision impact your life and the lives of everyone you come in contact with?

Create a plan: The same way you plan your vacation, create a well-defined plan for your future. Use the SMART criteria. Your goals should be Specific, Measurable, Achievable, Relevant, and Time-bound. With proper outlined steps, you can reach your envisioned destination.

Seek personal growth: Embrace the idea of continuous learning and growth. Understand that making mistakes is part of the learning process. They are opportunities in disguise to improve and invest in yourself before anything else. Learn through the help of books, workshops, and trainings, or with the help of coaches and mentors.

Take action: A plan without action is only a plan, a dream, not a reality. Make a commitment to be disciplined and proactive, and stay the course of action.

Be an example: Inspire others. Lead by example. Let the people around you see how you lead yourself effectively, through purpose and self-development.

TIPS TO BE HIGHLIGHTED

Serving is leading: Real leaders are in the service of the ones they lead. They are compassionate and know the needs of the people they are leading. Just like a ruler who lives amongst his people, prioritize the progress and growth of those you lead, and you will be the leader of choice.

Continuous learning: Strive for continuous growth and development. Seek improvement through feedback from others, identify areas for development, and embrace a lifelong journey of accumulating skills and applicable knowledge.

Values and integrity: Be trustworthy and true to all those you interact with. Build trust and reliability by keeping your commitments and not breaking them, even the ones you have to yourself.

THREE REFLECTION QUESTIONS

What is your vision for yourself?

_____

Think about your future:

Where do you want to go? Where do you want to be five years from now?

_____

How are you going to get there?

_____

This leads us to figuring out how to pave a path towards developing a leadership character. But first, we must delve deeper into the thought process of a leader mindset.

CHAPTER 4

BECOMING RESPONSIBLE

Understanding The Need For Self-Valuation

The reward that you get in life is in equal proportion to the service that you give. This refers to the intention behind what you can offer to create positive change. The greater the value of this intentional service you can provide, the greater the reward in seeing the change that you want to create.

Hence, we must constantly search for ways to increase our value by working on ourselves. This doesn't just mean expanding our knowledge base or being in touch with changing trends or the politics and economy of a country. It means improving our own mindset, which then creates an environment where others will benefit from our growth.

Your value does not increase by having more valuables. Owning a car, a big house, and other material possessions does not benefit others.

Your value increases by becoming more valuable. And becoming more valuable means the ability to create a vision that enables others to grow and build on their own visions and goals. As a leader, your vision creates a positive influence on others. However, many are not invested in building their future.

Over the years, I've asked hundreds of employees this question: 'Who is responsible for your career growth and your development?' And ninety-five percent of the time, I get answers like 'HR' or 'my manager' or 'the organization,' when in fact, the person responsible for your development and growth is you.

SO WHY IS SELF-DEVELOPMENT SO IMPORTANT?

In a long-running organization, often amongst the C-suite level, we have heard the words: 'We need a fresh pair of eyes' or 'We need to inject new blood to tap into innovative ideas.'

What does the top management really mean when they say we need to pump or inject new blood into the system? Does it mean that you, an experienced and seasoned employee, have no opportunity for future growth in the organization? That could be true. And that is exactly how I would have understood it.

However, it is essential to realize that there's a world of difference between new people and new thinking. New blood and a fresh pair of eyes refer to bringing in new people, whereas a fresh perspective implies new and innovative ways of thinking.

What do you think all organizations are in real need of? New blood or a fresh perspective? The fact is that the only reason they are getting new blood is for a fresh perspective.

So why don't you be the one to supply them with that fresh perspective? And how do you do that? The way to get a fresh perspective is to change the way we look at things. And to change the way we look at things is to change the way we think. To change the way we think, we need to constantly be learning and developing ourselves.

I remember a time when I was working in a well-known bank. I wanted to grow, to differentiate myself from others. I needed to learn a new skill, which was wealth management. I studied and sat for the exams but failed three times. The fourth time, I passed. Although I did not get the role of Head of Wealth Management, the knowledge added a lot of value to me as it broadened my outlook, and I received a bigger opportunity in the future that was suited to my experience, and the value-add was the wealth management knowledge.

The moral of the story is: No investment in yourself is wasted. Learn to keep tabs on the evolving world market. Our knowledge and learnings give us the flexibility to be ready and willing to change with changing times.

REFRESH YOUR PERSPECTIVES

Let's look at the great companies that have great products. Take Apple's iPhone as an example. Almost every year, they roll out a new iPhone with better and more developed features.

You need to have the same mindset when you look at yourself. You are your own product, so look at what needs to be upgraded or developed within. The sooner you come to terms with and embrace this reality, the sooner a journey towards successful leadership starts. It is critical for all products to keep developing and evolving as per market needs or they, and we, become obsolete.

Let's take BlackBerry as another example.

BlackBerry or RIM (Research in Motion), a leading software giant, gained fame with their smartphones that were introduced in April 2000. Due to how easy the phone made using the internet, along with its security features, it became a market leader in the mobile industry, with every corporate employee wanting to have a BlackBerry in their hand. Apple entered the market in the year 2007 as a competitor, only to be followed by the entry of Google's Android in the year 2010, both with new features and user-friendly touchscreen designs.

BlackBerry was slow to react to market preferences and it failed to adapt quickly to changing market needs, which led to its downfall in the mobile industry.

BlackBerry's failure to adapt to market changes and understand consumer preferences led to it neglecting the demand for user-friendly touchscreens and modern designs, and this failure was one of the main reasons for its decline as a market leader.

IDENTIFY THE ENDGAME

Whatever you want to achieve in life, start with the end in mind.

Answer the following questions:

Where do you see yourself in the short term, in one to three years?

Where do you see yourself in the long term, in three to five years?

_____

There are skills needed to achieve your short-term goals, and skills needed to achieve your long-term goals. When you clarify what they are, you will have greater clarity about your next step in that direction.

You need to constantly search for ways to increase the services that you are providing to become more valuable.

To share an example: Did you know that the average baby falls thirty-eight times a day before they learn to walk?

Success uses the same formula. Falling or failing is part of the journey to success, and falling does not make you a failure. Failing to get up, quitting, which is a deliberate mental choice, is when we become a failure. Those who choose not to be defeated will keep trying and will eventually walk in the shoes of success.

I will leave you to think about my next question. We never gave up on ourselves when we were babies. We were determined to be successful, to prove to ourselves and the world that we could do it, so why do we give up so easily now? What happened along the way, from the time that we were babies to now, that made our determination weak? Why do we sabotage our own aspirations?

What devastating blows have we encountered that have made us mentally, spiritually, and physically resistant to achieving greatness?

These questions help us understand our own inhibitions and resistance to developing or moving through the failed attempts and focusing on trying again.

To achieve great heights, we must first understand what holds us back and what lifts us up. The environment we live in and the people who surround us have a great influence on our ability to achieve our goals.

LEARNING HIGHLIGHTS

Becoming accountable and understanding the need for self-valuation is fundamental for both professional and personal individual growth, especially when it comes to leadership. Self-growth is the main asset that allows us to adapt to changing environments, and it also means that we have a mindset that makes us willing to see new ways of thinking and living. It stresses the importance of taking ownership and creating our own journey while continuously pursuing ways to advance ourselves.

The perspective of being your own product like Apple's iPhone, or failing to adapt to change like BlackBerry, highlights the need to constantly evolve, adapt, and innovate to stay with the times and ahead of the curve.

Encode this and cement your faith that you will have a proud legacy worth writing about.

My personal story regarding my own learning journey underlines the value of investing in oneself and embracing challenges. Failures are inevitable – everyone has felt a stab of failure – but the key is to learn from them and grow.

The analogy of a baby learning to walk reminds us that we humans are wired with perseverance and determination as part of our DNA, and it is critical to tap into these god-given marvels in order to achieve and amplify our greatness.

Lastly, recognizing the immensely powerful influence our environment and the people around us have on our journey is essential for making positive strides in our personal and professional lives.

Become an advocate of change: Encourage new perspectives and innovative ways of thinking with an open mind. Adapt to market and environmental changes. Be aware of your surroundings to stay relevant and successful.

Failures are teachers: See failures as wisdom gained. Investigate what went wrong and use those experiences as bridges to your future success.

You first: Invest in yourself before anything else. If you are not achieving, then note what needs to be improved, and put in the time to learn and grow.

Stay determined: Be as stubborn as a bull if you have to when it comes to your self-determination. Remember greatness is in your DNA. Be as determined as you were when you were just a baby learning to walk. Refuse to give up on your dreams or on yourself.

Become a value creator: Understand what it is you bring to the table and what it is that actually gets appreciated. Your worth is not defined by material possessions but by the value you bring to the world through your skills and services.

Continuously improve: Keep moving, keep evolving, and keep developing yourself like a world-class product to meet the demands of this ever-changing landscape.

Become accountable: Know that your career growth and development are your responsibility alone. Take ownership of your journey, and actively work towards becoming a master of your craft.

CHAPTER 5
ANCHORS AND LADDERS

Your Environment

According to a study by psychologists at Queen's University in Kingston, Ontario, the average human being has around 6,200 thoughts a day.

What if all these thoughts were negative? What if all these thoughts were positive? Are our thoughts in constant flux? Why do we think the way we do? And how do we overcome it?

> 'If your point of view is positive, you will see the challenges in the future as opportunities.'
>
> – HIS HIGHNESS, SHEIKH MOHAMED BIN ZAYED AL NAHYAN, PRESIDENT OF THE UNITED ARAB EMIRATES

The way we think and how we are influenced by our thoughts are concepts that appear in the age-old wisdom of almost every culture. The fact is, we are our thoughts, and often allow ourselves to be led by them. Almost all our behaviors and actions find their seed in a thought we once had or have.

THE SILENT INFLUENCE

Each and every person who enters our life, or is part of our world, brings with them their way of thinking. They have a contribution by adding value to our lives or by adding negativity. These people can be divided into two kinds: anchors and ladders.

Having friends who help you on your personal growth journey is one of the fortunes not everyone in this life is lucky enough to have. They are gifts. They are the ladders that give you a leg up when you need it. These people create an environment of growth and good mental health that accelerates your momentum on your path to success.

Ladders are the people who surround you with positivity. They have a natural knack for making you feel better, for keeping you in the zone of optimism. Such people are your cheerleaders.

If you do not have such people in your life, find such 'ladders.' Make the deliberate effort to make them part of your life.

ENVIRONMENT OF PEOPLE

We are molded by our environment – our beliefs and our motivations are affected by those we associate with on a daily basis. We are affected in ways we don't even realize.

An analogy for how we are molded by our external environment can be found by looking at watermelons. Watermelons are ordinarily oval in shape. However, the Japanese have come up with the square-shaped watermelon.

In 1965, a Japanese farmer, Yamashita, began the development of square watermelons. An entire decade was spent studying and experimenting with different cultivation techniques, including using containers for molding, which led to the invention of the first square watermelon around 1975.

Growing a square watermelon is relatively simple. While the watermelon is still growing on the vine, it is placed into a transparent square box that is smaller than the watermelon's size at maturity, making the watermelon grow and mold into a square shape as it takes up the same shape of its new environment.

We don't realize how much our environment affects us. A study shared by Codie Sanchez on her YouTube channel involved an experiment conducted on individuals during fifty thousand hours of work in eleven companies. It showed that if an individual sat within twenty-five feet of a top performer, that person's performance increased by fifteen percent. On the flip side, if a person sat twenty-five feet from poor performers, their performance suffered by thirty percent.

This is clearly an important part of our lives we need to take into account. Who is influencing us without us realizing it?

The way to achieve your goals in life is to make a conscious effort to be surrounded by the kind of people who already have achieved their goals for themselves. Never ask advice from a person who you would not be willing to trade places with.

Darren Hardy, in his book *The Compound Effect*, refers to research done by social psychologist Dr. David McClelland of Harvard. He claims that our reference group determines as much as ninety percent of our success or failure.

Steer clear of negative people, as negativity breeds negativity, turning you into a negative person. How does this happen? Over many months and years, in small doses, you are fed their way of thinking, and this leads to a negative mindset. These thoughts become habitual and feed into more such thoughts. This creates a domino effect on the mind until the mind transfers this negativity to our bodies and it starts affecting our health and wellbeing.

Our perspective, the way we look at things, affects our relationships. We begin to experience self-doubt, and this, in turn, impacts our financial decisions. As we become colored with negativity, we miss out on opportunities. We get so blinded that we cannot recognize an opportunity even if it stares us directly in the face.

CREATING A MINDSET

I like to share a fable to elaborate on how the environment affects our identity.

In a time not too long ago, there lived a happy-go-lucky shepherd in the vast expanse of the Indian forest. Like all hard-working shepherds, he spent his days watching over his flock and carrying out his duties without a worry in the world.

One fine day, the shepherd decided to venture deeper into the forest, taking an alternative route rather than the way he usually strolled. He entered into a denser area of the forest to gather wood for the cold nights, and while doing so, he stumbled upon quite an unusual sight. A lion cub, abandoned and alone, lay there hurt, whimpering in pain and confusion. Fear struck the shepherd's heart, as if he was stabbed, for he knew that where there is a lion cub, there must surely be a mother, a protective lioness, nearby.

Subconsciously, the shepherd's survival instincts kicked in as his heart started to palpitate faster. He carefully retreated without making a sound, his senses heightened and his body trembling with fear, and watched from a distance. As the world stood still and time stretched into eternity, the shepherd saw a pack of hungry wolves getting closer. The shepherd's heart filled with guilt about the innocent young cub, and without a second thought, he ran forward and scooped up the cub into his arms. Pressing the cub gently against his chest, he ran towards his village as fast as he could.

Days turned into months, and months into years, and the lion cub grew among the sheep. The shepherd even named it Tommy. Tommy became one of the flock, playing and sleeping with the sheep, and even started eating grass.

Life was good for Tommy, but one stormy night, an unexpected turn of events took place. Tommy was woken by the sound of a strange growl echoing in the darkness. Anxiously, Tommy turned his head, only to see a pair of fierce, bloodshot eyes – it was the biggest, most fearsome creature that Tommy had ever laid eyes on. It was a black wolf.

Fear ran through Tommy's veins. At first, the wolf was also afraid to see a lion, but when it saw the lion trembling and could smell his fear, it approached the lion. The wolf stated its intentions very clearly. 'I shall visit you every fourth night, and with every visit, I shall take with me a sheep as my rightful dinner. Should you even think of interfering, you shall bear witness to my wrath and feel my deadly claws pressing into your fluffy fur, you overgrown pussy cat.' With that terrifying threat, the wolf left and took along with it a prize to devour, leaving Tommy shaken and terrified.

The wolf returned, fulfilling its ruthless promise. With each visit from the wolf intensifying Tommy's fear, the wolf made sure to fuel Tommy's belief that he, too, could become the wolf's next target. And each time, the wolf reminded Tommy that he was nothing but an overgrown pussy cat, and sometimes even meowed and kicked him just to keep him in his place.

Then, one fateful night, luck shined on Tommy and the sheep, as there was another lion searching for food just outside the village. The lion, in hunger and frustration, roared, which woke up Tommy, and he went to see what the terrifying sound was. Not far away was the wolf, and as Tommy saw the wolf, he hid behind the trees. As soon as the wolf saw the lion, thinking it was Tommy, he started taunting and meowing at it. 'Hey, pussy cat, what has brought you here today?' The lion turned around and tore the wolf apart in seconds and dragged his carcass deep inside the forest.

As the lion walked away with the dead wolf in its jaws, Tommy looked at the lion with a tear rolling down his mane. He said, 'Oh God, I wish, in my next life, that you make me a lion.'

ANCHORS AND LADDERS

Underestimating the influence of those around us, on our ambitions and our energy, can be disastrous. Such people act as anchors, tying us down, shackled and stuck. Eventually, they drown us in their unfulfilled lives. The chaos and drama that they bring with them start to act as energy stealers and bandits that rob us of all positivity and dreams, leaving a dark cloud above us at all times, and the only thoughts that we end up with are negative ones. They are troublemakers.

One of my best friends used to say, 'It is no use. You will never get a shot at the big roles, as you do not know the right people, and you do not associate with them.' He was so right, as I was with a negative person who could only find reasons why I could not succeed. Isn't that a sobering thought?

How many of these people do you have in your life?

It could be, sadly, anyone – our best friend, spouse, siblings, parents, or even our child. It could be someone who we are not even aware of, a mere blip on our radar, but has a colossal impact that is draining us of all ambitions. The worst part is that we are not even aware of the damage that they are causing, intentionally or unintentionally.

It is vital in your search for excellence that you steer clear of negative individuals.

ANCHORS AND LADDERS

Once I'd had enough, I said, 'You know, what I actually need is a mentor.' And I went and found one, and I was surprised that the same person I thought was a roadblock for me actually mentored me when I asked him to. He helped me discover all my blind spots and develop the necessary skills to reach new heights and level up.

One of my mentors taught me a valuable lesson. I was studying in the UK at Oxford University for an intensive leadership program. It was December, and the temperature was minus 7°C – freezing conditions. I was falling sick often. For dinner, we went to town, which was around seven to ten kilometers away. After dinner, my mentor said, 'Let's walk back.' It was at least a forty-five-minute walk. Reluctantly, I agreed.

As we walked, he asked me a question: 'Why do you think you are freezing and falling sick?'

I looked at him. 'Because of this cursed weather!'

He said with a smile, 'No, Ahmed. There is no such thing as bad weather, only bad clothing. If you had done your due diligence and checked the weather conditions before coming here, you would have prepared with the appropriate clothing and shoes, just as I have done. And you would actually be enjoying this weather.'

The next day, he asked me another question: 'What did you learn from yesterday?'

I simply replied that there is no such thing as bad weather, only bad clothing. He said, 'Wrong again. To be a great leader, you need to learn how to look into the future and forecast outcomes based on the studies and statistics available. Only by looking into the future can you start planning today.'

This wisdom has stuck with me ever since. When we blame external situations, we must realize that we cannot change the externals, and we need to be prepared for them.

ANCHORS AND LADDERS

The below table defines some of the characteristics of Anchors and Ladders.

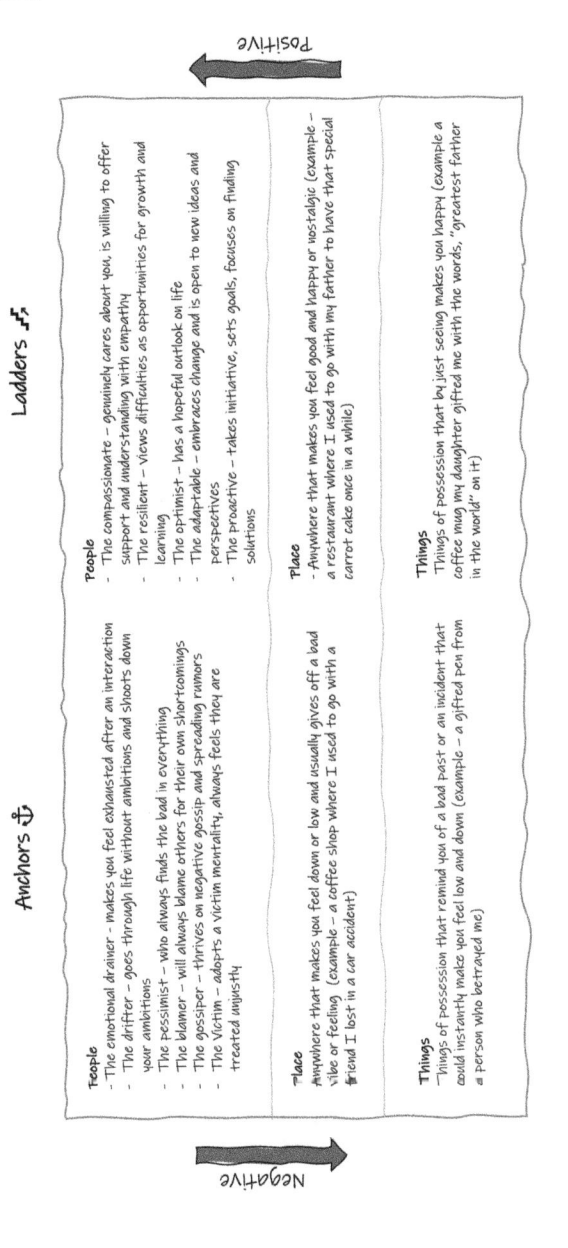

← Positive

Anchors ⚓

People
- The emotional drainer – makes you feel exhausted after an interaction
- The drifter – goes through life without ambitions and shoots down your ambitions
- The pessimist – who always finds the bad in everything
- The blamer – will always blame others for their own shortcomings
- The gossiper – thrives on negative gossip and spreading rumors
- The Victim – adopts a victim mentality, always feels they are treated unjustly

Place
Anywhere that makes you feel down or low and usually gives off a bad vibe or feeling (example – a coffee shop where I used to go with a friend I lost in a car accident)

Things
Things of possession that could instantly make you feel low and down (example – a gifted pen from a person who betrayed me)

Ladders 🪜

People
- The compassionate – genuinely cares about you, is willing to offer support and understanding with empathy
- The resilient – views difficulties as opportunities for growth and learning
- The optimist – has a hopeful outlook on life
- The adaptable – embraces change and is open to new ideas and perspectives
- The proactive – takes initiative, sets goals, focuses on finding solutions

Place
- Anywhere that makes you feel good and happy or nostalgic (example – a restaurant where I used to go with my father to have that special carrot cake once in a while)

Things
Things of possession that by just seeing makes you happy (example a coffee mug my daughter gifted me with the words, "greatest father in the world" on it)

→ Negative

Based on the above table fill in your Anchors and Ladders.

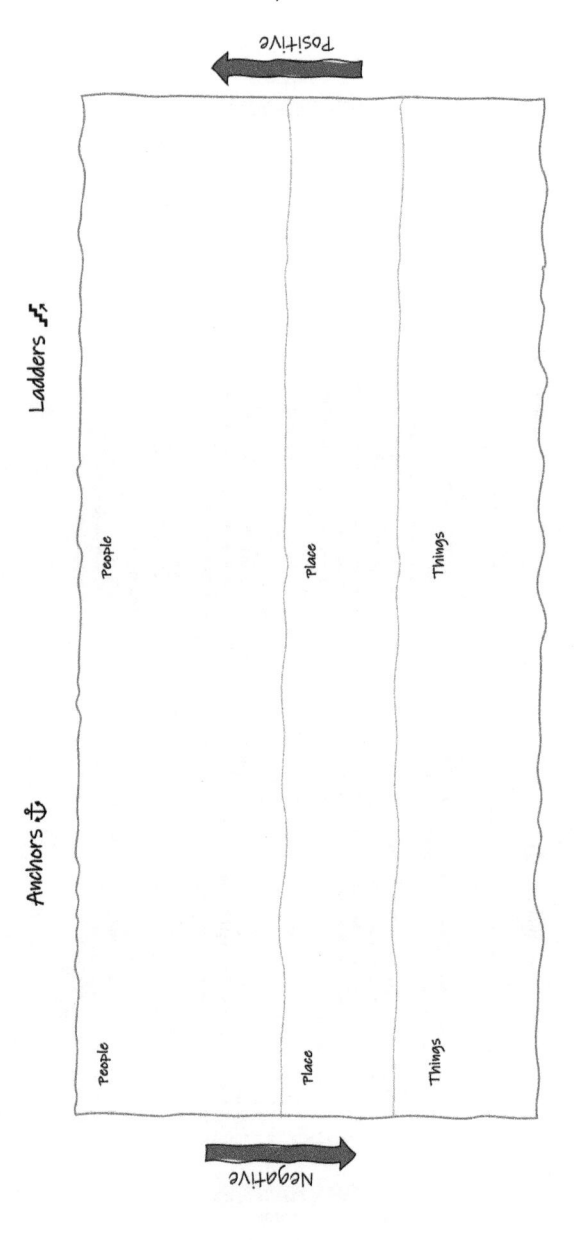

← Positive

Ladders ↗		
People	Place	Things

Anchors ⚓		
People	Place	Things

Negative →

ACTION POINTS

Be proactive in shaping a positive and growth-oriented environment for yourself. Clearly identify the anchors and ladders in your life. Deliberately maximize your time with the ladders that boost you up and minimize your exposure and time with the anchors. Seek out coaches, mentors, positive influencers, and like-minded or more positive-minded individuals who can help you gravitate towards your destination and chief aim.

REMEMBER, YOU BECOME YOUR ENVIRONMENT!

Your environment has the most powerful influence over your thoughts, actions, and overall wellbeing.

> If there is <u>one thing</u> that can change the course of your life and if there is only one idea in this book that you want to <u>apply to your life</u>, it should be the deliberate creation of your own environment through the identification of your <u>Anchors & Ladders</u>.

Once we figure out what holds us back and what inspires us to move forward, we can then discover how to plan and select our goals.

CHAPTER 6
GOALS AND PLANNING

How To Select Goals And Create An Action Plan

A New Year's resolution is not a goal. No tracking, no accountability – just a spur-of-the-moment decision. Sooner or later, the warmth and excitement of New Year's Day will fizzle out, and by the end of the month, the resolutions have lost their luster.

THE TIME IS NOW

By the end of this chapter, you will understand the relevance of both short-term and long-term goals, and how to map them out.

There are short-term goals, which are to be achieved in one to three years, and there are long-term goals, which are to be achieved in three to five years. Both are important for the other. Short-term goals that are connected to your long-term chief goal have the most impact on your future.

This was one of my goals – to write a book of around 40,000 words. That was my long-term chief goal. My short-term goal was to read for one hour a day and listen to audiobooks while commuting back and forth. And then record ideas that popped up from the many books that I consumed. I kept a recorder with me at all times. You never know when you are going to have a eureka moment!

Then, I planned to write a thousand words each weekend, and doing this was interconnected with my main goal.

Each week, if I achieved my short-term goal, I felt I was getting closer to my chief goal. It became my strategy to finish writing the book, a roadmap to reaching my destination.

We do not have a wide spectrum of timelines in this life. What we do have are three timeline periods: the past, the present, and the future.

Do you want a better future? Are you willing to pay the price?

Yes, my friend, sacrifices will need to be made. Nothing is free in life. Everything must be paid for. The only thing that changes is the means of payment. For a better future, you must pay for it with your present. You must invest in yourself and your goals, and pay through learning, development, and the hard work that you put in today for a better tomorrow.

Tomorrow's coming, whether you like it or not. Where you were three years ago is not the same place where you are today, nor will it be where you are three years from now. Do you want to leave it to chance, or do you want to choose your destination?

The main catch, however, starts with how you pay for your future with your present. And for that, you need to be in the present, not hanging onto the past. You cannot say, 'Why did I not get the promotion?' or 'Why is that person better than me?' You need to abolish this overwhelming guilt. You need to be aware of a potential better you and have a clear goal and vision of where you are going without letting mistakes and disappointments of the past blur your vision.

The Greek myth of Sisyphus tells of a Greek king who was cursed by Zeus to spend all eternity in the underworld, where he would be tasked with pushing a boulder up a hill, only to see it roll back down every time he neared the top, never to gain success.

In the same way, clinging on to past mistakes and disappointments is like carrying a heavy burden that distorts your vision and hampers your progress. By releasing this burden, you can clear your mind and sharpen your focus, enabling you to see new opportunities and embrace the potential of your future.

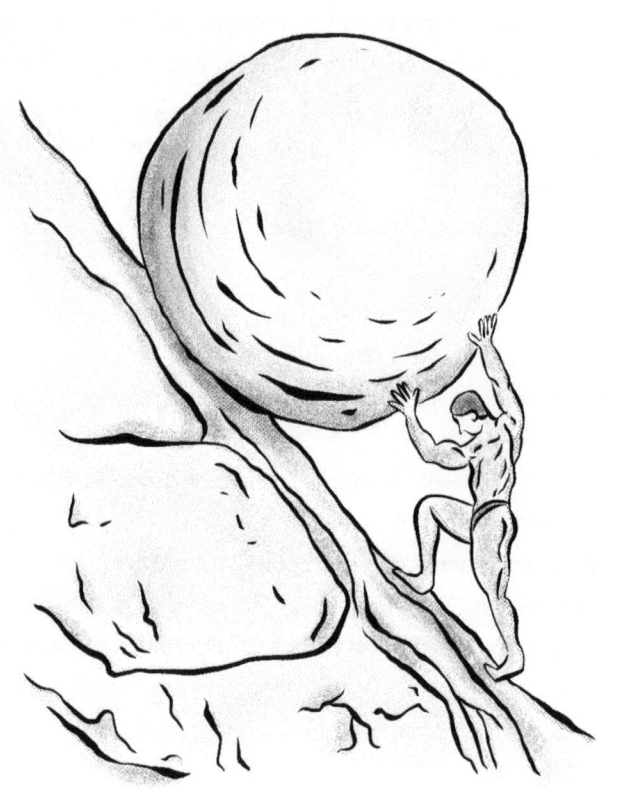

You need to ask yourself the following questions and write down the answers:

What goals and dreams do you most desire to achieve?

Your answer: _____

Why?

Your answer: _____

'The person who has a clear, compelling, and white-hot burning WHY will always defeat even the best of the best at doing the how,' says Darren Hardy, author of *The Compound Effect*.

Why is it important to work from a plan or even have one? Working from a plan not only gives you direction but also motivates you while supplying you with positive energy. One of the key reasons some individuals achieve more than others is that they have clear plans. The greater the clarity regarding what you want and when you want it, the easier and less time-consuming it becomes to get.

Author and time management guru Brian Tracy writes in his best-selling book *Eat The Frog*, 'Only about 3% of adults have clear written goals. These people accomplish 5 and 10 times as much as people of equal or better education and ability, but who for whatever reason have never taken the time to write out exactly what they want.'

By now, you should have a clear vision, backed by a burning desire to go for your goal. Once you support this with a solid, thought-out plan, then execution might not be easy, but it most definitely will be a joy ride.

CHAPTER HIGHLIGHTS

Goal-setting and the creation of a plan to achieve them is not a casual exercise and should not be taken lightly. Have your plan written down in a place where it can be reviewed periodically and changed, based on your circumstances. As long as the goal remains the same, the plan can take multiple forms.

This goal-setting and planning mechanism is the foundation for the creation of a successful and fulfilling future. Short-term goals that are aligned to your long-term chief goals are what drive us daily toward our vision and dreams.

Invest in your future by forgiving yourself for all your past mistakes. I say here *forgiving* not *forgetting*. Learn from your mistakes to become stronger and better, but if you are too focused on what has passed, you are not in the present, and when you are not in the present, you will become negligent of your future, as to invest in your future, you need to pay for it with the time that you have today.

ACTIONS FOR YOU FROM THIS CHAPTER

What is your burning desire?

Answer: _____

What goal will give you satisfaction if you achieve it and a sense of pride and purpose?

Answer: _____

What new skills are you going to start learning that will take you towards your chief goal?

Answer: _____

Write down your vision for yourself clearly below:

Answer: _____

FINAL WORDS

Stop grappling with your past mistakes, look forward with an optimistic can-do attitude, open your mind, and unlock the wide spectrum of opportunities that is within you, set your goals, create your plan, take action, go for it, apply discipline, and turn your dreams into a reality.

CHAPTER 7

MASTERING YOUR CRAFT

Applicable Knowledge Is Power

Do you want to be known as a jack of all trades and master of none, or do you want to be known as a master craftsperson?

By the end of this chapter, you will understand what specialized knowledge means, why it is important, and how it is attainable.

They say knowledge is power, but the real power is applicable knowledge, knowledge that can be applied, that can be transformed into an action plan or a roadmap that takes us towards our vision and goal – that is power.

REFINE YOURSELF THROUGH KNOWLEDGE

Applicable knowledge is critical if we want to succeed and become great leaders. We are only as valuable as the service we deliver to others, and the level of service that we deliver is totally reliant on the knowledge that we have of our craft. This is why the knowledge that we acquire, that we go after in life, should always be applicable, specialized knowledge. Successful leaders from all walks of life never stop learning, never stop acquiring skills that are related to their craft.

> *'The way that you become rich is not by wishing your life was easier, but instead by focusing on making yourself better.'*
>
> *– JIM ROHN*

Applicable knowledge, like success, is not achieved through a desire for an easier path. It is attained by gaining the mastery to effectively tackle tough and grueling problems and situations by developing the necessary skills and abilities to confront anticipated challenges. That said, one of the fundamental keys to growth and success is devoting oneself to continuous learning and self-improvement in your selected craft.

One of the fastest ways of gaining applicable knowledge is through mentors and coaches. Finding the right mentor or coach is one of the greatest self-investments for development that will enable you to reach new heights.

To further elaborate on this, let's look at it from a new angle by putting on a different pair of lenses. Have you ever known of a world-class heavyweight or Olympian gold medalist without a personal coach? We are all individuals, and the same applies to us. So why is it okay or good for them but we don't do it for ourselves?

Anyone who wants to go beyond mediocrity and be at the top of their game in their chosen field requires coaching and mentoring.

Gary Keller and Jay Papasan write in their book *The ONE Thing*, 'It's never too soon or too late to get a coach.' Commit to achieving extraordinary results, and you'll find that a coach gives you the best chance possible.

Another way of becoming a great leader and acquiring applicable knowledge is by reading books and learning from authors who are renowned gurus in your particular field of interest. 'Reading gives knowledge, creativity, power, satisfaction, and relaxation. It cultivates your mind by exercising its faculties,' said Earl Nightingale.

Reading a book is the same as learning from a person's experience and gaining their wisdom for yourself.

EXPONENTIAL KNOWLEDGE

I'm a numbers person, and so to make things simple, I do the math. Say you read ten books a year over five years, and each book has been written by a master craftsman, a guru in the field, with an average of twenty years of experience that he or she has poured into writing their book, and after reading each book, you grasp or benefit only two percent of each book, which is three or four pages.

The math?

A. 2% of 20 years (240 months) equals 4.8 months of experience per book.

- 240 x 2% = 4.8

B. 4.8 months of experience times 10 books a year equals 48 months.

- 4.8 x 10 = 48

C. 48 months (4 years) of learned experience plus 12 months of self-experience equals 5 years of experience gained in one year.

- 48 + 12 = 60 months (5 years)

D. 5 years of yearly gained experience over 5 years equals 25 years.

- 5 x 5 = 25

So if you read 10 books a year for the next 5 years, you will be giving yourself 20 years of experience from the gurus of the world in your specific chosen field, which will make you a master of your craft and a guru yourself.

Brian Tracy, bestselling author, speaker, and business consultant, has over thirty years of experience and has written over seventy books. He states, 'If you read fifty books in a particular field, it can be equivalent to earning a PhD.'

My preferred way of gaining experience and learning is through reading and making notes in books and writing down what I have read so that I can go back and look at the points I found useful again. You are probably thinking, 'This is too many books to read' and 'Who has the time?' Well, you can still gain knowledge. If you can't find time to read, then try audiobooks.

I found that listening to audiobooks, along with my reading, helped me a lot. In fact, I have read and listened to over 150 books regarding leadership in the past four years, and sixty of them were audiobooks I listened to while commuting.

By listening to an audiobook for one hour a day, you can listen to an average of one book per week. That is an average of fifty books a year. How many people do you know who could say that they have completed more than fifty books in a specialized field? And if they have, are they not subject matter experts?

It is easy to say you have no time to read, but if you make the time, you will benefit greatly.

Tip: Do keep a recorder handy and take voice notes while listening to audiobooks.

Ask yourself two questions:

1. How many hours a week do I commute or drive alone in the car?
2. Isn't it worth investing one hour a day in myself by listening to audiobooks in my field of expertise, which will eventually have a positive impact on my thoughts, career, and life? Isn't it worth it?

TRANSFORMATION THROUGH AWARENESS AND FEEDBACK

Another way of self-development is by becoming aware of the blind spots that we have, and this could come through feedback. This is a strong form of applicable knowledge that many people take for granted or tend not to look at.

Feedback comes in many forms. Usually, the feedback that we talk about is the feedback that we give. While doing so, it is essential to provide specific feedback about the task, not the person. We can address areas that need improvement and not criticize the weaknesses.

Feedback is essential to improve our work and measure our progress. Without our customers' feedback, we cannot work effectively in serving them as we would not know if we are performing well, what needs to remain the same, what needs to be changed, or if we are getting better or worse.

Good leaders understand the value of feedback and use a 360-degree feedback system on a yearly or half-yearly basis, which helps them understand how they are perceived by their stakeholders within the organization and by outsiders.

However, the golden rule when asking for feedback is that it is essential to be open-minded and avoid getting defensive. You should listen to the advice that makes sense and encourage other people to share constructive feedback. This is done by treating everyone with respect and giving them a safe space to speak candidly.

Remember, this feedback is for your development to uncover your blind spots. The less sugarcoated the feedback, the better for you, and the more you can work on the areas that will make you a master craftsman.

360 feedback

```
Coach/Mentor    Boss
         ↘     ↙
Ladders →   YOU   ← Boss's Peers
Mentees  ↗   ↖   ← Your Peers
         ↗    ↑
    Subordinates   Your Peer's
                   Subordinates
```

Learning is a lifelong journey of growth in your field. Leaders never stop learning, even after they become world-class masters of their craft.

CHAPTER HIGHLIGHTS

The gathering of general information will make you an interesting person, but not a master. Seek specialized knowledge through mentors, coaches, and books written by experts in your field. This will take you to the next level, making you part of the elite few. Mastery over applicable knowledge in your chosen field is the only true way to become an expert in your craft.

'To become a master, one must learn from a master.'

Continuous learning is crucial for growth and self-improvement. Identifying blind spots through feedback is essential for personal and professional development. Make continuous learning a lifestyle.

No master or expert ever stopped enhancing their expertise and skills. This is the hallmark of a true leader.

It may seem challenging to find the time to learn during our busy lives, but finding ways to prioritize will pay off in abundance. By dedicating ourselves to obtaining applicable knowledge, we can attain mastery at its highest level in our chosen field and stand out as an exceptional leader, fulfilling all our visions and goals.

Remember, power – real power – does not lie in knowledge but in the way this knowledge can be applied towards becoming a true master craftsperson.

TIPS FOR MASTERING YOUR CRAFT

Identify three mentors:

1: _____

2: _____

3: _____

Send emails or call them and ask them to become your mentor. Write down the date that you will do this.

Date _____

Make a list of the books that you are going to read in your field this year to gain applicable knowledge.

1: _____

2: _____

3: _____

4: _____

5: _____

6: _____

7: _____

8: _____

9: _____

10: _____

11: _____

12: _____

MASTERING YOUR CRAFT

Make a list of the audiobooks that you will be listening to while commuting to work

1: _____

2: _____

3: _____

4: _____

5: _____

6: _____

7: _____

8: _____

9: _____

10: _____

11: _____

12: _____

Use the 360-feedback system, and write down the date.

Date _____

Create your learning grid: Add the learning grid to track your learning progress, including books read/listened to, coaching or mentoring engagements and feedback, 360-degree feedback received, and actions taken based on all feedback along with progress.

Finally:

Remember, true mastery comes from applying the knowledge you have gained by turning it into action. Start and take your first step today.

You will question the need to keep track of all of the above. Indeed, everyone is pressed for time. And almost everyone will say, 'I don't have the time.' To counter that excuse, let me share a time-check methodology that I have personally found effective.

CHAPTER 8

TIME-CHECK PRIORITIES BY TIME-BLOCKING

Multitasking And Distractions

To manage your time effectively, you first need to know where you're spending it.

No one can control time, as we cannot increase or decrease time. What is in our control are the activities we do in the time we have. We all have the same amount of time no matter who we are or what we do.

By the end of this chapter, you will get a deeper understanding of how we can work with time and not against it, becoming a master craftsman on the path to achieving more in less time.

PRIORITIZING

All great leaders work from a plan and know exactly what is important. They know which tasks to prioritize and which ones to delegate or deal with later. That is the art I want you to craft.

Look at your plan, list the tasks and projects, and ask yourself: If there was only one thing that you could do, what would it be? What one thing would add the most value to you? And rank the tasks in that order.

Delegate or eliminate all tasks that you know are not the top one and can be done as well or better by someone else.

In becoming a master craftsman, the path to more is through less time spent.

It is important to put some thought into this and write down ten things, if done extremely well, without a flaw, that would make you an extraordinary individual. Now take a good look at that list and cut it in half. Pick the five things that will make the biggest difference in your life if you achieve them this year.

Take those five items, and think about which one, if done perfectly, would be just as important by itself without achieving the other four. Rate this item the highest.

Follow this method and rate numbers two to five. The first item or number one item or task should be part of your daily workday practice or routine, and on the last day of the week, progress is to be reviewed by you. For items number two and three on your list, review their progress biweekly.

Items number four and five can be delegated and reviewed once a month, or be eliminated if possible.

PRIORITIZE TASKS

During COVID-19, I changed jobs. As things started to settle down with the pandemic, work was chaotic. Suddenly, everything became urgent. In a single day, we had around five meetings where all my direct reports and some of their direct reports were attending with other departments and sometimes even other entities. Although everyone was busy and doing a lot of work, actual output and productivity were low.

I asked each of my direct reports to chart down and share with me all the meetings that they were attending throughout the week. This was then shared and discussed with all of them collectively in a meeting. I know – another meeting?! But at this meeting, I asked them to simply identify and write on a whiteboard what were the top five objectives of the organization, rating them from highest to lowest in terms of impact and weight. Then I asked each of them to write down on a piece of paper five of their top objectives, which, if delivered, would have a positive impact on the organization's objectives.

I had ten direct reports, so if we do the math:

10 x 5 = 50. Correct?

Wrong! In reality, although the total number was 50, many objectives overlapped, and we ended up with a total of 33 objectives.

Then, we rated these objectives:

The top 10 as A.

11 to 20 as B.

21 to 33 as C.

We redistributed the 33 objectives, making sure that everyone had an A, B, and C. There was clear accountability and no overlapping to cause dilution of the task due to internal dependencies and having more than one owner.

Some got four, some three. I still remember giving one person only two objectives, but both were As.

We then set some rules:

Objective A was to be delivered with no milestones or deadlines missed and would be done by each staff member themselves with weekly updates.

Objective B was to be delivered on time, although a small amount of slippage would not be frowned upon, and would be managed by each staff member with a biweekly update to be shared.

Objective C was to be delegated to their top staff member, reported on monthly, and no one would turn a blind eye when it came to timelines.

Overall, the daily meetings came down from five a day to one, sometimes two for each team member, and productivity went up. This was the result of taking the right strategy with the right resources. Everyone was not required to do everything. We had specialized focused groups, and in the process, the situation became less chaotic, leading to lower stress levels.

Rules of Prioritization

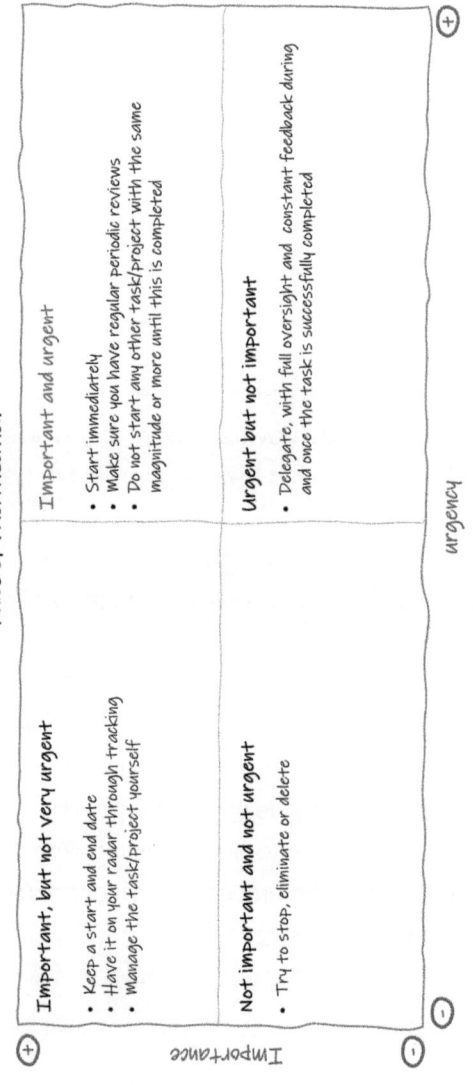

Important and urgent
- Start immediately
- Make sure you have regular periodic reviews
- Do not start any other task/project with the same magnitude or more until this is completed

Urgent but not important
- Delegate, with full oversight and constant feedback during and once the task is successfully completed

Important, but not very urgent
- Keep a start and end date
- Have it on your radar through tracking
- Manage the task/project yourself

Not important and not urgent
- Try to stop, eliminate or delete

Importance / *Urgency*

TIME-CHECK PRIORITIES BY TIME-BLOCKING

Based on the table on the left fill in your urgent tasks and projects

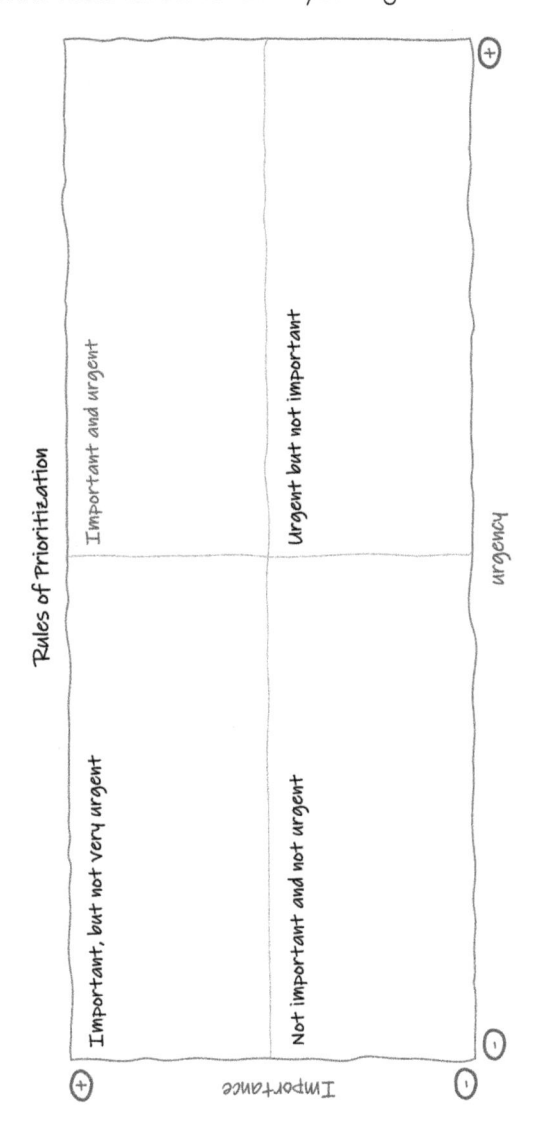

Rules of Prioritization

- Important and urgent
- Urgent but not important
- Important, but not very urgent
- Not important and not urgent

Importance / urgency

A LEADER'S LEGACY

STRATEGIZE TEAM EFFORT

Success is not achieved by the person who does the most tasks. It is achieved by the person who does the tasks that have the greatest impact.

Since not all tasks hold equal importance, and some are more critical than others, it is more productive to focus on completing the most important tasks first. Identify the two or three tasks that will make the most significant difference when completed and prioritize them. The most important tasks are those that will create the results that will be significant in your goal-achieving plan.

Block out time in your calendar to work on these two or three most important tasks each day, dedicating an hour or two in the morning to tackle them. Be on a do-not-disturb mode. This will help you maintain an attentive mindset and allow you to stay focused. Beware of non-critical interruptions that will divert your attention. Ignore all distractions. Blocking time early in the day and completing the most critical tasks will leave you with free time to handle anything that comes your way during the day. You will experience a sense of accomplishment as you progress closer to your bigger goal.

This planning will greatly benefit from a time check.

TIME-CHECK PRIORITIES BY TIME-BLOCKING

The below is a sample grid that shows exactly how much time I spend on which tasks a day.

Time Check Table

#	Items/Tasks	Hours per week	%	Remarks
1	Driving From / To work	17	10%	Listening to audio books, regarding leadership, mastering my craft one book at a time, completing 1 book a week.
2	Sleeping	56	33%	One third of most adult lives are spend sleeping.
3	Screen time (Phone)	16	10%	Daily average of two hours and forty minutes, need to bring this down and spend my time more wisely.
4	Exercise	4	2%	One hour four times a week
5	Self Development (reading, studying)	3	2%	Reading thirty minutes a day before bed, 1 book every ten days.
6	Writing	3	2%	Write over the weekend two x 90-minute blocks.
7	Weekly - self reflection	1	0.5%	One X 60-minute block on Friday, see if I have achieved all my past weeks goals and what will I be planning for next week.
8	Work	40	24%	Five days a week 8 hours a day
9	With Family & Friends	16	10%	Saturday, other than reading at night, full day for family no need to look at the time switch off from the world and reboot for next week.
	Total Hours	156	93.5%	👍 168 Hours / Week = 100%

Based on the above table fill-in your own Time Check

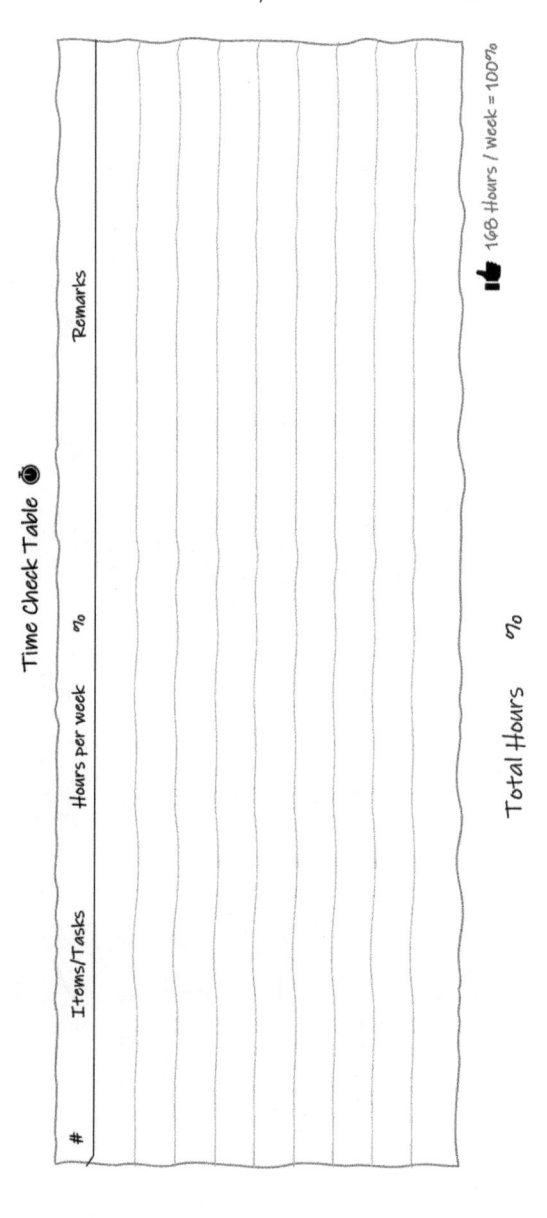

Time Check Table 👁

#	Items/Tasks	Hours per week	%	Remarks

👉 168 Hours / Week = 100%

Total Hours / %

Ask yourself the following questions.

Which of these activities adds value to me?

Which of these activities hampers my growth?

Which of these activities makes me happy?

Which of these activities could be done just as well or better by someone else that I could delegate or outsource?

Which of these activities can I spend less time on?

Which of these activities should I stop?

Which of these activities should I do more of?

TIME-BLOCKING

Make a weekly checklist, starting from the last day of the week. Work towards it, and strike through every task done. Time-block ninety minutes every last day of the week to reflect on, review, delete, or move incomplete tasks to next week. But be careful not to overdo it with your expectations. Master prioritizing and deprioritizing.

Time-Blocking – Daily slots

#	Time	Tasks	Occurrence
1	5 AM	Wake up	Daily x 5 Times a week
2	8 AM	30 Minutes Email Review	Daily x 5 Times a week
3	9 AM	20 Minutes Social Media	Daily x 5 Times a week
4	10 AM	90 Minutes Deep Work	Daily x 5 Times a week
5	12:30 PM	30 Minutes Emails	Daily x 5 Times a week
6	3:30 PM	30 Minutes Pending Items	Daily x 5 Times a week
7	4:00 PM	60 Minutes reflect on the week and plan next week	Every Friday
8	10:00 PM	Go to bed *(Hard to commit)*	Daily x 5 Times a week

TIME-CHECK PRIORITIES BY TIME-BLOCKING

Based on the table on the previous page, create your own daily time-blocking schedule.

#	Time	Tasks	Occurrence
1			
2			
3			
4			
5			
6			
7			
8			

Time-Blocking – Daily slots

SELF-REFLECTIONS

1. What am I going to do at work next week to increase my value and the customers' satisfaction?
2. Have I done what I said I would do last week?
3. If not, why not?
4. Do I drop and replace the task or finish it this week or next week?

If anything has been brought forward three times, drop it, or study how important it is and if it is worth having on your time-blocking list.

SCHEDULING

Another way to use time-blocking and become more productive is to have a fixed schedule for time-blocking.

TIME-CHECK PRIORITIES BY TIME-BLOCKING

See the sample schedule below, which is easy to use in your Outlook calendar.

Time-Blocking – Outlook Calendar

Legend: Low Priority | Medium Priority | Mid-High Priority | High Priority

Mon	Tue	Wed	Thu	Fri	Sat	Sun
1 Item 1 Item 2 Item 3	2 Item 1 Item 2 Item 3	3 Item 2 Item 3	4 Item 1 Item 2 Item 3	5 Item 1 Item 2 Item 3	6 Item 1	7
8 Item 1 Item 2 Item 3	9 Item 3	10 Item 1 Item 2 Item 3	11 Item 1 Item 2	12 Item 1 Item 2 Item 3	13 Item 1	14 Item 1 Item 2
15	16	17	18	19	20 Item 1 Item 2	21
22 Item 1 Item 2 Item 3	23 Item 1 Item 2 Item 3	24 Item 1 Item 2 Item 3	25 Item 1 Item 2	26 Item 1 Item 2 Item 3	27 Item 1	28 Item 1

(Days 15–19 marked as Vacation)

To get productive, make sure the time-blocks are in your calendar. During those working times, keep your phone on airplane mode and switch off all distractions. No social media. No calls. No one to come and speak to you. No phone notifications. No emails. No requests from anyone. You will be amazed at how much work you can get done within ninety minutes with full focus and no distractions.

According to Cal Newport's research, the ninety-minute time-blocking method can improve productivity by up to thirty percent.

By now, you know how much I love numbers, so come on, let's do the math. Now, if we take my suggested approach and add two time-blocks to our daily workday routines, in theory, we would be 300 percent more productive that week. Too good to be true? Okay, let's break it down.

A: 90-minute time-block twice a day, 5 days a week, equals 10 time-blocks a week.

- 2 x 5 = 10 (10 time-blocks per week)

B: 10 (x 0.3) = 30% (percentage of increase of productivity as per the research done by Cal Newport) equals **300%!**

- 10 x 30% = 300%

Hey, what I'm saying here is give it a try. I did, and I was blown away.

MULTITASKING

I first started time-blocking, or *deep work* as it is called by author Cal Newport, after realizing how much of my time was wasted by distractions and interruptions.

It felt like I had no time to work due to sudden interruptions and having to go through emails when they dropped into my mailbox. Thanks to our smartphones, even in the middle of lunch or a meeting, we keep checking our emails and sometimes our social feeds. Reminders or keeping a to-do list in my notebook began to look more like a laundry list. The only time I used the calendar was when someone sent me a meeting invite, so it was more of a passive or reactive approach, not a proactive one.

I started time-blocking and using my Outlook calendar with notifications on. I scheduled my entire week, from my meetings to my writing, to my gym times, dentist's appointments, break times at work, checking emails, and more. I even had appointments set up with myself for weekly reflection and to work on my two biggest objectives at work. By doing this, not only was I able to have more focus and get more work done, I actually found out that we have so much extra time that we are not utilizing at all!

Applying this time-blocking technique may take some getting used to. But just like riding a bike, once you master this skill, you will retain it and your productivity will shoot through the roof. The true art of productivity through time-blocking is fairly simple:

- Identify your tasks.
- Start at the end of the week to fill your calendar for the next week.
- Block-time to work on tasks based on their priority.
- Keep a weekly measurement for yourself as a target – say, writing 1000 words a week.
- At the end of the following weekend, after a week of having time-blocked your calendar, have a reality check to see if the tasks are getting done in the allocated time. Are you meeting your targets or was the time too stretched? Do the tasks need some adjustments – or to be replaced or deleted?
- Switch off from all tasks for one full day to reboot your brain.
- Start over.

MULTITASKING FAILS

It's time for us to, once and for all, debunk the myth that multitasking gets more done. The simple exercise below is taken from the book *Scrum* by Jeff Sutherland and slightly altered by me to bring this message across.

TIME-CHECK PRIORITIES BY TIME-BLOCKING

Multitasking Exercise

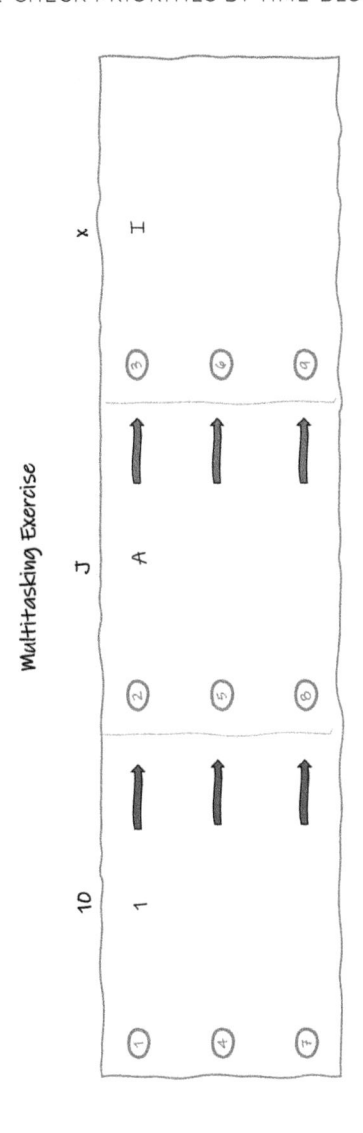

Above is an example of an exercise that you will be doing to debunk multitasking. The exercise is simple. First you would need to use a stopwatch and time yourself. As soon as your time starts, fill in the below table from left to right starting with the number one (1)

then the letter A, then the Roman numeral one (I), until you reach 10, J, X.

Write down how many seconds it took you!

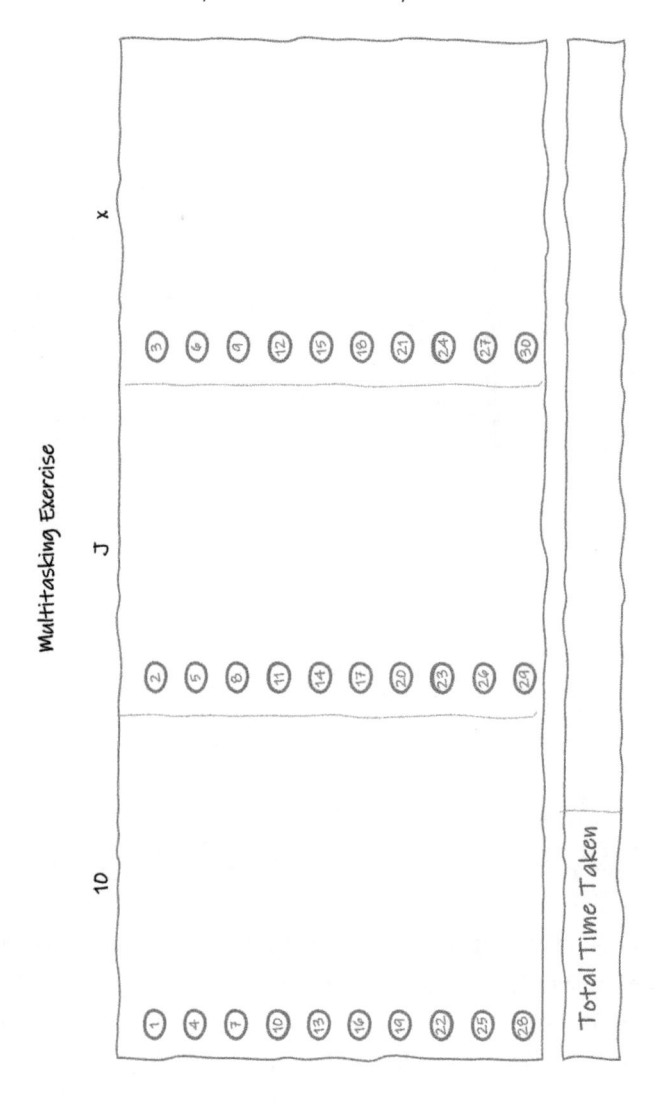

Multitasking Exercise

10 — ① ④ ⑦ ⑩ ⑬ ⑯ ⑲ ㉒ ㉕ ㉘

J — ② ⑤ ⑧ ⑪ ⑭ ⑰ ⑳ ㉓ ㉖ ㉙

X — ③ ⑥ ⑨ ⑫ ⑮ ⑱ ㉑ ㉔ ㉗ ㉚

Total Time Taken

TIME-CHECK PRIORITIES BY TIME-BLOCKING

Now using the same concept as above you will, instead of writing from left to right, you will write from top to bottom finishing each column before moving on to the next.

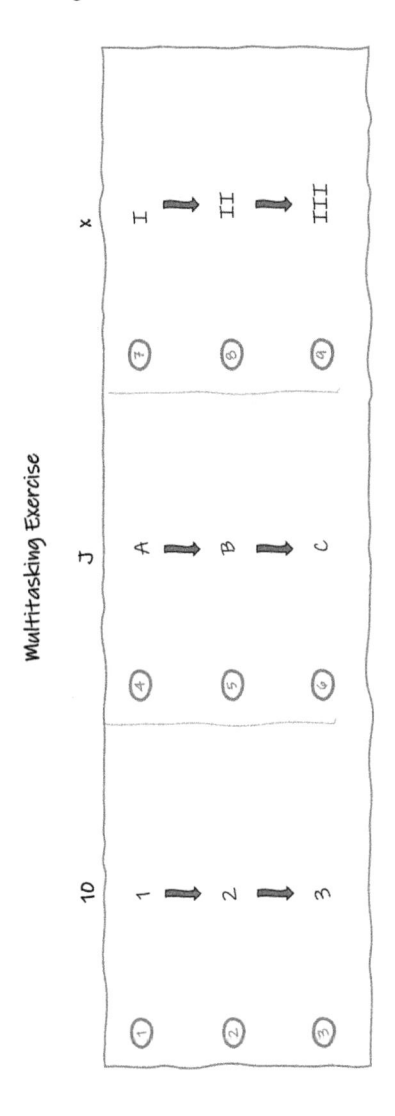

Multitasking Exercise

x:
I ➡ II ➡ III
(7) (8) (9)

J:
A ➡ B ➡ C
(4) (5) (6)

10:
1 ➡ 2 ➡ 3
(1) (2) (3)

As you can see from the above example you will start with the first column and write down from 1 – 10, then move to the next column writing A - J and finally moving to the last column writing I – X.

Ready, Set, Go!

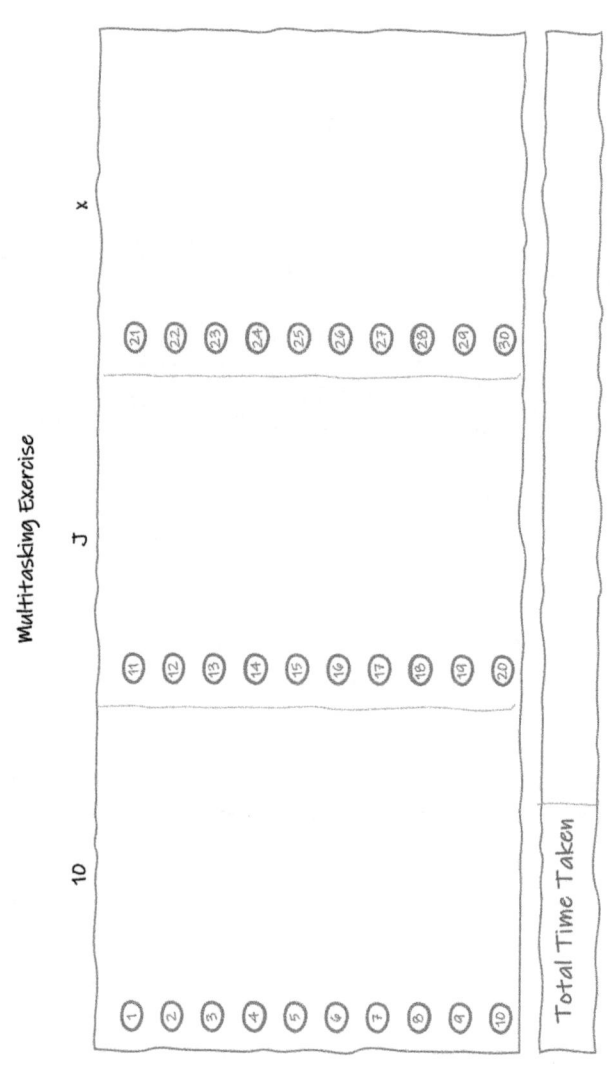

Multitasking Exercise

1 2 3 4 5 6 7 8 9 10	11 12 13 14 15 16 17 18 19 20	21 22 23 24 25 26 27 28 29 30
10	J	X

Total Time Taken

How many seconds did it take you?

Multitasking is actually switching between tasks too quickly. One way we tend to multitask is to speak on the phone while driving a car – with the speaker phone on and trying not to look at it. Driving a car due to constant repetition becomes as habitual as brushing our teeth, and we still have accidents due to this. Hence, I don't recommend you attempt to multitask while driving.

Evidence shows that if multitasking was doable, we would have no road accidents reported due to texting and driving. Driving needs your full attention, and texting not only takes our eyes off the road but diverts our attention to reading and replying to texts.

The fact is that after years of repetition, when we can do a task without thinking, we don't need to use much brain power, and that's why we think we are multitasking. But when we need to focus, it is impossible to do two tasks at the same time.

The Russian proverb states that 'a man who chases two rabbits catches none.' The wisdom behind it is that if a man tries to chase two goals at one time, he may fail to accomplish both.

Keep track of your multitasking habits and reflect on whether you are able to get things done faster, or if it is resulting in more strain on you.

DISTRACTIONS

Not only do distractions hamper your professional life, they have a way of sneaking up and lingering around your personal life. If we are not careful, our work life overflows into our personal lives through emails that we can easily access on smartphones.

I recall I was spending time with my son, and he was upset because I missed his school sports day. I regretted that I didn't get a chance to watch him play on the basketball team and apologized, hoping he would forgive me for missing the event. He talked about the game with real excitement and was telling me how well he played. However, I heard the ping of an email and noticed it was from my CEO. Something urgent had come up. I became distracted and felt the compulsion to respond to the CEO right away. My son was talking, and after I finished my email, he was just looking at me as if he was waiting for an answer, so I asked, 'What's up?'

He said, 'Well, what do you think? Whose mistake was it?'

At this point, I felt lost, and anyone could make out that I did not have a clue what he was talking about.

Disappointed, my son went to his room without saying another word.

Later, I found out that he quit the team, and to date, I do not really know what happened.

This personal life experience proved two things to me. First of all, you cannot multitask. Secondly, distractions have a way of getting into your life. Be aware of your surroundings or you will miss out on the most beautiful moments in your life.

Some advice. When at work, work. When at home, give your family the time they need – switch off all email notifications and focus on your loved ones. I am very careful to be attentive when I am with my son or any family member. We have a bond, and I am careful to not let work affect my relationship with them.

As we journey through life, we are faced with many issues, and some of them can come in the form of personal problems that distract us from our dreams and goals. Managing these inner distractions is an art and a very doable one. First and foremost, we must change the way we view these disruptions.

Write down the problems. Usually, they are much bigger in your head than in reality. Now break them up and start to categorize them into two strands:

1. Tasks
2. Circumstances

Circumstances are not within your control, and you have no influence over them. Hence, you cannot change them, just as you cannot control the weather.

On the other hand, certain activities are within your control. You can make a difference in your own life by making them a habit – for example, going to the gym. By starting to refer to those inner interruptions as tasks, we can approach them with the mindset that since it's a task, there is a solution and you can take action to solve the task at hand.

Circumstances cannot be changed by our actions. They must not be given much thought since you have no control over them.

An example of a circumstance is when you have a wonderful dinner planned with a very dear friend of yours in the outdoors, a very nice setting with candles to create a romantic mood, and one hour before your dinner, it starts raining and is getting heavier by the minute. This is a circumstance. You cannot control the weather. You cannot do anything about it. So why entertain the feeling that you are responsible for this plan failing? Why dwell on it? Why get distracted by it?

The only thing that you can do is either postpone your candlelight dinner or maybe go to the movies. Change your plans, but don't give too much energy to 'should have been' as that will distract you, drain your energy, and create a sense of disappointment, which then will take you off track.

This perspective helps us focus on what we can control rather than getting caught up in things that are beyond our influence. Trying to fix circumstances is a waste of time and energy.

There are five steps you can take to change your view of a distraction and deal with it as either a task or circumstance.

1. Write all your problems down on a piece of paper. By now, you should know that I write everything down. I'm an advocate of writing. It makes more sense when we see the problems in writing, bringing clarity to our thoughts.
2. Categorize them either as a task or circumstance.
3. Delete all items that are identified as circumstances.
4. Write all the tasks on the left. And on the right side, find solutions for the tasks.
5. Take action.

Since time cannot be controlled, the only thing that you can control is how you manage your activities in the time you have. Performing these activities well requires you to manage your attention, have laser-sharp focus, and cut out all distractions. Becoming a master means not only doing and practicing the right things but also not doing the wrong things that pull you back and take you away from your goals. Distraction keeps us buried and adds fuel to one of the deadliest enemies of progress: procrastination.

IN CONCLUSION

Effective and efficient time management involves understanding the fact that time is not under anyone's control or command; however, what we can control is how we utilize the time we have by prioritizing activities and tasks that are essential for achieving our desired success in life. Hence, having laser-sharp focus on the most important activities transmutes into the most significant results, along with time-blocking, which is a game-changer for anyone who knows how to use it in the right fashion. This will support us to shine and stand out among all our peers as our productivity will shoot through the roof.

The idea that multitasking is a positive is a myth. True productivity comes from focusing deeply on one task or activity at any given time.

Breaking down problems and categorizing them into tasks or circumstances helps us focus on what is within our control and switch to a solution-oriented mindset, instead of simply worrying.

Managing our attention by eliminating distractions and stopping unproductive habits while putting aside chunks or blocks of time can help us become masters of productivity.

CALL TO ACTION

Be in charge of your tasks, activities, and projects.

Become a master of productivity.

Start by evaluating how you spend time currently and recognize areas where you can make the maximum positive impact.

Prioritize your tasks based on their importance.

Create a time-blocking schedule to allot focused time to your key activities. Practice the ninety-minute time-blocking method to boost your overall performance and get more quality work done in less time.

TIPS FOR EFFECTIVE TIME MANAGEMENT

The key thing about effective time management is understanding that it is about doing the right things with precision and focus; it is not about doing more. By mastering these techniques and gaining these skills, you unlock higher productivity levels, all while reducing stress, which enables you to chip away at your long-term goals in a more efficient manner with little to no procrastination issues along the way. Take action now. Transform your approach to time management and become a leader of yourself.

PART 2

LEADING OTHERS

When a leader embarks on a path that is of a visionary, he inspires and influences others to develop themselves. A true leader is one who can guide others to become great leaders.

CHAPTER 9
CULTURE

Creating Cultures That Vibe

Powerful leaders transform strangers into an unbreakable tribe while eliminating the bad apples. Leaders do more than issue instructions to a group of people. They also inspire, mentor, and communicate values to them. You will learn the importance of a leader's responsibilities towards culture, and how to create a culture that vibes.

To be a great leader, you need to be the best at creating great teams by creating a great culture. The word 'culture' originates from the Latin word *cultus*, which means care, cultivation, and worship. Over time, the usage of the word evolved to include customs, beliefs, and practices of a group of people.

POWER OF CULTURE

Leaders build connections among team members by keeping things simple and positive and making sure there is a high level of communication. Leaders face their teams with the truth without sugar-coating anything and help them find a way to learn and grow. It is critical that you make sure everyone has a voice.

As a leader, one of your main pillars for success is the culture that you create, develop, or maintain. Daniel Coyle writes in his book *The Culture Code*, 'Group culture is one of the most powerful forces on the planet. We sense its presence inside successful businesses, championship teams, and thriving families, and we sense when it is absent or toxic.'

Multiple studies have shown that a strong culture can have numerous positive effects on an organization, and it's linked to:

1. **Employee retention:** Strong cultures boost employee retention rates as the employees feel connected to the organization.
2. **Productivity:** Strong cultures have staff engaged and motivated, which leads to higher productivity.
3. **Innovation:** A strong culture helps foster a more creative atmosphere as staff feel more comfortable sharing new ideas.
4. **Brand reputation:** The values and mission of the organization are clear and felt internally and are also reflected externally, which translates into a positive reputation.

A research project conducted by two professors of the Harvard Business School, James Heskett, UPS Foundation Professor of Business Logistics, and John Kotter, Professor of Leadership, looked at the corporate cultures of more than 200 companies with strong organizational cultures. These companies grew net income by 756 percent, compared to the one percent for the companies lacking in culture.

An inseparable part of any leadership is the development and maintenance of a strong and aligned culture, which is critical in driving business success, achieving strategic goals, and creating employee satisfaction.

How do we create a strong culture?

1. By understanding the difference between the wants and the needs of your team and your own.
2. By having clear, measurable accountability and ownership.
3. By having a clear message on the environment that you want.
4. By being transparent.

5. By making everyone feel important.
6. By making everyone feel safe.
7. By removing the bad apples.
8. By not wasting each other's time through unnecessary meetings.

As a leader, you are accountable with prejudice not only for your team and its output but also for the environment and culture. Behavior that brings negativity and disturbance should not be tolerated.

WANTS AND NEEDS

As a leader, you need to identify and meet the needs of the people that you lead – *needs* and not *wants*, as what they want might not be what they need. Wants are wishes or desires – they are a goal, a destination – and needs require discipline to get there. You cannot be disciplined for anyone but yourself. That is not your responsibility, and as the old saying goes, 'You can lead a horse to water but you cannot make it drink.'

A need is a tool, a vehicle, a psychological requirement, and without it, one cannot achieve their wants, goals, desires, and necessary outcomes.

My want is to become a leader, but you cannot promote me to a leadership position and automatically expect me to be an efficient leader. A manager also knows, as a positional leader, there's a difference between a manager and a leader.

As my leader, your job is to identify the leadership skills that I *need* to acquire along with the tools and resources that will help me develop these skills, which, in turn, will transform me into a leader.

Managers vs Leaders

How do they	Manager	Leader
Manage Talent?	Use	Develop
Approach Mistakes?	Blame	Learn
Set Directions?	Tell	Challenge
Make Decisions?	Decide independently	Consult, involve the team
Get things done?	Control	Support
Communicate?	Give instructions	Communicate openly with active listening
Influence?	Through authority	By inspiring
Empower?	Closely supervise	Delegate authority

WANTS AND REWARDS SYSTEM FOR YOURSELF

Create a wants and rewards system for yourself by following these two simple steps:

1. Write down five wants for this year.
2. Write down five rewards that you will give yourself for being on track.

The wants should be something like:

1. Reading twelve books that relate to your field for the year – that's one book a month.
2. Losing fifteen kilograms.
3. Becoming knowledgeable of my content on social media.

You get the idea. These are wants that are within your control. Now you need to break down these wants into weekly tasks or activities, create a simplified road map with intervals, and reward yourself every time a milestone has been achieved.

Rewards can be tricky. Sometimes, we can ground ourselves by not doing the activities that we take for granted or have become part of our habits or weekly tasks and instead do something like go to the movies or on a boys' night out.

CULTURE

RESPECT OTHERS

I used a technique that helped me to focus and create a change in my environment. I came up with a motto for myself. You can create your own motto. Put it up in a place where everyone can see it, and they will know what you stand for.

For example, I had a motto posted where everybody could read it. In one of my work areas where I felt a lot of negative vibes, I made

> We believe in family values and anyone who does not behave like a family member with one another or the customer is not welcome in our house.

a big poster and put it on the wall next to the coffee machine. It stated, 'We believe in family values, and anyone who does not behave like a family member with one another or the customer is not welcome in our house.'

Do this to build awareness.

Send an email to the entire team. Ask them, 'How can we make our workplace a place where we would happily work and not move to another organization even if it offered double the salary?'

Everyone is equally important. As a leader, you need to remember that, and you need to stand for that. All human beings have a fundamental need to feel important. It does not matter if it is a customer, coworker, friend, or even a child. What matters is that they feel respected, appreciated, and heard. The more important they feel around you, the more they will value their relationship and time spent with you, and the more they will behave in the same manner, and this great culture will flow down to everyone in the building.

SO HOW DO YOU, AS A LEADER, BUILD A STRONG CULTURE?

We've spoken a lot about culture, but how do we build a strong culture? What does it mean? What would you do? How could you do this? The answer: The same way you build a family. Why family?

It is simple. If you ask any group of successful people where you see flourishing relationships – be it at work, in a football team, or among business partners – to describe their relationship with one another, you will hear one word, and that word is 'family.'

You will hear people say 'We feel like a family,' but what does that actually mean? Breaking it down to its core, family means trust, and no human emotion is stronger than trust.

So how do we build trust?

Through safety.

SAFETY

When I speak to my brother, no matter what the subject, and no matter how wrong or right I am, he listens with care and does not judge me, which makes me feel safe. I am safe to make mistakes, speak my mind, and express my feelings without being judged or punished. This kind of freedom to express one's self and vulnerabilities creates a more positive environment conducive to the interchange of feedback.

Do you have a feeling of safety among your team members, your direct reports, your peers, and with your boss?

To build a great culture, your first job is to build a feeling of safety around your team. They have to feel that you are there to protect and guide them through anything and everything. Safety comes with the feeling of belonging, the feeling of being heard, the feeling of being cared for, and the feeling that you matter.

When this feeling of safety doesn't exist, a person becomes aloof and feels that they are not wanted, that they are not part of a group, a team, or a tribe. Your job as a leader is to identify who is not feeling safe with the team by asking yourself this one question:

'Who in my group does not feel safe and connected?' Now, write those names down.

Speak with them one-on-one. Find out why they do not feel safe and connected, and fix it.

Teams are made up of individuals who trust and look out for each other. They collectively form a successful team. As pieces of a puzzle, all play a role in reaching excellence. For you to gauge the person who does not feel safe and understand them better, you need to ask them, 'What would it take for you to be pleased to be part of this team?'

If you sense that you cannot fix this person's mindset and the employee is going to cause problems for the team, your job is to let him or her know where you stand. You need to be open about the consequences if the employee does not improve. This may even mean that you have to warn the individual that you will have to let them go if their unwarranted behavior continues.

Always think about the culture that you are trying to cultivate, and do not tolerate weeds within your cultivation.

However, it is important that you are able to accurately distinguish and understand the difference between gossip and bad news. The culture should not be one of 'my way or the highway' or of giving only good news and hiding all the bad news, as that could backfire. That is the opposite of safety and could result in a disaster.

No one likes to be the bearer of bad news, and most people try to avoid giving bad news and feedback, but without this vital information, how can we become better? Bad news is a bit like bad weather. As mentioned before, there is no such thing as bad weather, only bad clothing.

So when we do get bad news, let's do our research and find out what the weather is and what it is going to be, so we can prepare for it. In fact, we can learn to find the positives in the experience, be it cold, hot, rainy, sunny, snowing, or stormy.

When we learn what went wrong or what is coming that might be equal to a storm, we can prepare for it – sometimes by cutting our losses, and sometimes by turning it into an opportunity.

We all know that the COVID pandemic was bad news, but some pharmaceutical organizations and other industries flourished through supplying medications, gloves, masks, COVID test kits, and other accessories related to helping people face the pandemic. This was an opportunity, and they were able to make use of this time by being prepared.

The ideas can come from all directions. Being open to them is also part of a leader's ability to take into consideration all possibilities.

Have you heard the saying 'Do not shoot the messenger'? In fact, no matter how outrageous, this person needs to be listened to carefully and made to feel safe. The individual who shares the whole truth without sugar-coating becomes an example for others to follow. To start speaking up, they should all feel that under your leadership it is okay to share bad news and know for a fact that everyone is safe.

TIPS FOR DISCOURAGING GOSSIP-MONGERING

As a leader, you must be aware of your surroundings and be aware of the unproductive, the lazy, and the unambitious staff who engage in idle gossip, who attack the weaknesses of others, or who attack staff who are trying to make a difference. Although small in number, gossipers are a deadly force to reckon with.

When dealing with such individuals, be careful how you proceed.

In the first instance, confront the gossiper directly and have a one-on-one conversation. If there is a repeat of the bad behavior and you notice that there is no change in this person, have another session, but this time, document it.

Effectively build a safety culture that offers top-down cover, and create an environment where people take care of each other. Your followers need to have trust in you and believe that you have their best interests at heart. As their leader, you should act as a shield for them during tough times and be willing to take accountability. This creates a sense of protection and a safety net, which cultivates an environment that fosters open communication and allows the exchange of ideas to flow freely.

When it comes to morale and productivity, as the saying goes, 'One bad apple can spoil the entire bunch.' These individuals destroy not only other individuals they engage with but entire teams by injecting doubt and worthless distractions that add no value. The only way to teach staff how to cut them off from the roots is by using this two-step simple technique.

Step 1: When someone comes and starts to gossip, ask them the following questions:

A. Does what you are telling me add any value to the team or the organization?
B. Where and from whom did you get this information?
C. Have you spoken to the person that you're speaking to me about?

Step 2: Switch from questions to actions.

A. I need you to go and have a conversation with the person you are speaking about, and then come back and give me an update. Let me know how it went.
B. Next time, I will call the person, whoever it may be that you're speaking about, and I will need you to repeat what you have been saying in front of that person.

As soon as these bad apples know that you will be asking them to confront the individual they are gossiping about, they will stop coming to you with gossip. This technique of dealing with gossipers should be taught to your direct reports. It should be known that you do not tolerate gossip in your team.

While you are doing this balancing act, you are at the same time obliged to give credit and celebrate little wins. Acknowledge and recognize success while taking responsibility for failures. This approach will have people eager to follow you. They will trust you to not misjudge or doubt their words. They know that you are committed to creating a healthy and positive work environment and that you will look out for them.

TIME WASTERS

Meetings are one aspect of office culture that wastes the most time and drains the most energy. According to the Harvard Business Review, 71% of senior executives say that meetings are inefficient and unproductive.

One of the best definitions of why we have meetings at work was penned by Peter F. Drucker in his book *The Effective Executive*. 'We meet because people holding different jobs have to cooperate to get a specific task done. We meet because the knowledge and experience needed in a specific situation are not available in one head but have to be pieced together out of the experience and knowledge of several people.'

How many meetings have you been to where multiple wonderful ideas have been discussed and numerous actions were agreed upon but none of them saw daylight? Why did that happen?

People leave without a firm conclusion about who will be responsible for what and by when. Common mistakes are having no assigned schedule, tracking, or responsibility given to a certain person.

The most time-tested method to get tasks done is by regularly tracking progress, but that can only be done if the people who are attending the meeting are open to healthy conflict and are willing to address the elephant in the room. In most corporate cultures, we see peers agreeing with each other and trying to avoid conflict at all costs.

So why are these meetings a waste of time, and how are they hurting your leadership?

One of my main issues with meetings with any new team is that no-one wants to call out the elephant in the room or everyone wants to agree with everyone so that the team does not hurt each other's feelings. That's why I always have four meetings a year with my direct reports to conduct an exercise, and I encourage them to do the same with their teams. This is where I induce conflict – these kinds of meetings I call 'the Boxer's Club.'

The format is simple. All my directs are contenders or boxers. Each takes the stand, and everyone has permission to have a go at them or throw a couple of hooks and jabs – not literally, just with words. I am the referee and make sure there is no punching below the belt or getting personal.

The aim is to encourage conflict in a way that makes each unit leader aware of all their blind spots and what they are doing wrong according to the rest of the team. By uncovering his or her blind spots, we are able to make them better leaders and stronger team members. This enables people to call each other out, with all their downfalls, without being personal or feeling bad. Everyone is well aware that this is the main aim of the meeting, which not only shines the light on their weaknesses but also helps the team connect on a deeper level, as they understand this is being done not to make anyone look bad in their boss' eyes but to help them grow and develop. The name – Boxer's Club – helps remove the unease of telling the harsh truth to their colleagues.

Steps to follow to make this a success:

- Call it the Boxer's Club.
- Explain at the first meeting why you have called it the Boxer's Club.
- Explain the rules.
- Take turns. All of them are to take a swing at one person, and each one will also be a 'target.'
- No one is to argue or defend themselves. This is not a matter of who is better or worse.
- All must understand that this is the perspective of the person who is taking a swing at the team member.
- Ask for examples. No comments are to be made that cannot be backed by facts or figures.
- The boss – that is you – is not to participate or give any comments.
- Have someone send minutes of the meeting that clearly mention each person's area of development.

- After three months, have another session with the same staff to review if any progress has been made in the area of development for each person.
- Find new areas, and do it all over again.

This has helped me bring the teams closer as it works as an icebreaker, and everyone actually starts to trust one another more. There is no speaking about one another behind their backs. They have a chance to say things openly to each other's face, basically killing gossip among your directs while developing them through candid feedback from their peers.

BACK TO BASICS

Indulging in meetings that result in no definite outcomes negatively affects your leadership by hurting your team's productivity. The simple solution is to avoid having unnecessary meetings.

The true cost of meetings is in terms of productivity.

Say you schedule a one-hour meeting and invite, for example, ten staff members to join this meeting.

One hour multiplied by ten staff members equals ten man-hours of productivity plus the minimum time each staff member takes to prepare for the meeting. For that, you could add an extra one to two hours.

You are trading a minimum of twenty to thirty hours of productivity for this single hour of a meeting – you better make sure the meeting is worth it.

Since meetings are a part of corporate life that you cannot totally dismiss, here are some rules of engagement for conducting an efficient and effective meeting:

- Never attend or call a meeting without receiving or sending a clear agenda. (Why are we having this meeting? What is the purpose? What is the expected outcome?)
- Make sure the people who will be attending will be able to add value. There is no need to have more than one person from each team attend. Sometimes, we see the manager and two or even three of his subordinates attend the same meeting, which is not acceptable unless it is for an announcement and is not a recurring business meeting.
- Set a start time and an end time on a phone. When the alarm rings, the meeting is over – it is a hard stop.
- Invite as few people as possible and make sure they are people you know will lead to a constructive outcome or a plan.
- Do not let people bring laptops. All devices are to be on silent mode. If anyone needs to present a PowerPoint, they should send their presentation before the meeting to the gatekeeper (the person keeping track of time and making notes).
- End with a solution and action plan that will be circulated and tracked, with each action point to have the person's name next to it who will be held accountable with timelines.

CULTURE

This is a sample of a highly effective meeting template that I personally use.

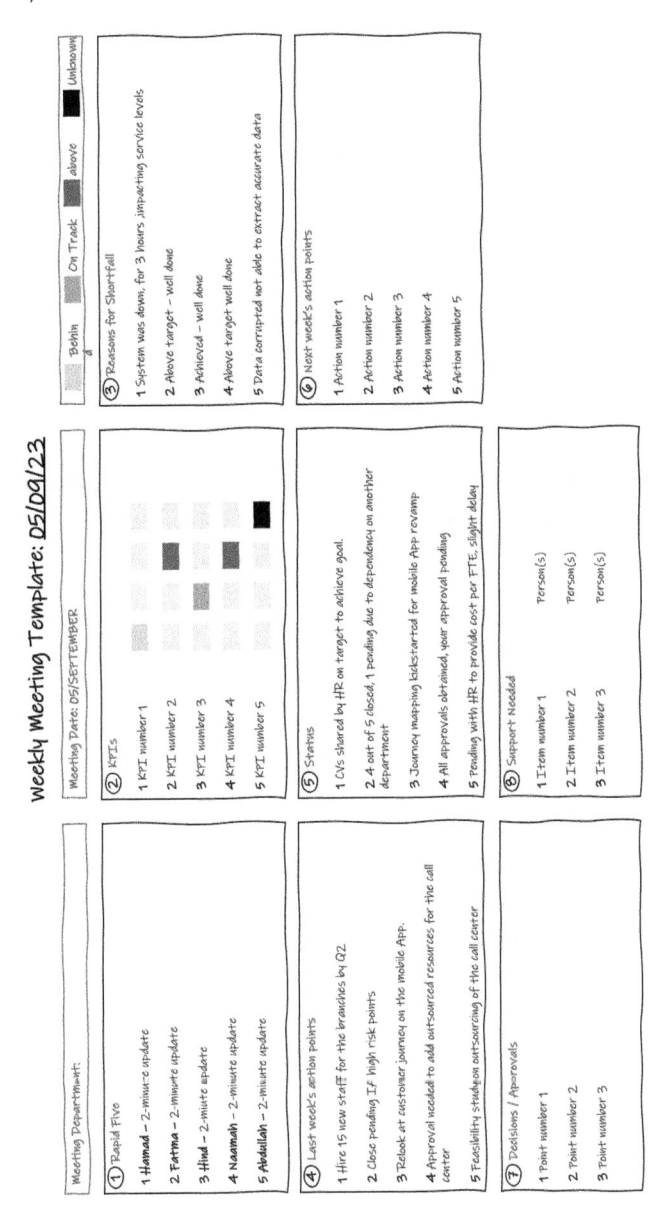

Weekly Meeting Template: 05/09/23

Meeting Department:

Meeting Date: 05/SEPTEMBER

Legend: Behin | On Track | Above | Unknown

① Rapid Five
1. **Hamad** – 2-minute update
2. **Fatma** – 2-minute update
3. **Hind** – 2-minute update
4. **Naamah** – 2-minute update
5. **Abdullah** – 2-minute update

② KPIs
1. KPI number 1
2. KPI number 2
3. KPI number 3
4. KPI number 4
5. KPI number 5

③ Reasons for Shortfall
1. System was down, for 3 hours impacting service levels
2. Above target – well done
3. Achieved – well done
4. Above target well done
5. Data corrupted not able to extract accurate data

④ Last week's action points
1. Hire 15 new staff for the branches by Q2
2. Close pending IT high risk points
3. Relook at customer journey on the mobile App.
4. Approval needed to add outsourced resources for the call center
5. Feasibility study on outsourcing of the call center

⑤ Status
1. CVs shared by HR on target to achieve goal.
2. 4 out of 5 closed, 1 pending due to dependency on another department
3. Journey mapping kickstarted for mobile App revamp
4. All approvals obtained, your approval pending
5. Pending with HR to provide cost per FTE, slight delay

⑥ Next week's action points
1. Action number 1
2. Action number 2
3. Action number 3
4. Action number 4
5. Action number 5

⑦ Decisions / Approvals
1. Point number 1
2. Point number 2
3. Point number 3

⑧ Support Needed
1. Item number 1 — Person(s)
2. Item number 2 — Person(s)
3. Item number 3 — Person(s)

The culture of meetings starts from the top, and it is your job to stop the bleeding of positivity and motivation. Ultimately, you are creating a family environment, a culture where people respect one another, and all are there to look out for each other and for the betterment of the organization.

CHAPTER HIGHLIGHTS

Being a leader gives you and only you the power to transform strangers into an unbreakable tribe by creating a solid and positive culture.

Embrace your responsibility to build the connections amongst your team members, promote mentorship, and communicate values. Your deliberate actions can make a significant impact on the overall satisfaction of the employees, which will have a flow-on effect on your organization and customers.

TIPS TO ACTION

Have clear, measurable accountability and ownership for all.

Clearly communicate the environment and culture you want to foster.

Be transparent, fair but firm, and open with your team.

Remember, every team member has a right to feel important and valued.

Prioritize creating a safe family-like environment where everyone can freely express themselves without the fear of being judged.

Remove toxic team members that hinder the culture's growth.

Eradicate unnecessary meetings and ensure all meetings have clear agendas with pre-defined outcomes.

Remember, trust and safety are two sides of the same coin and are equally important in building the foundation of a successful culture.

Act as a shield for your team. Celebrate the small and big wins, and take ownership of failures. Under your leadership, everyone must feel protected, listened to, and valued.

Remove all elements of gossip, like a farmer weeds and nourishes the crops, and encourage open communication.

Prepare for unseen challenges and turn them into opportunities.

Ensure you cultivate a family-like environment within your team, where trust and a sense of belonging thrive.

CHAPTER 10

RINGS OF INFLUENCE

Your Role As A Leader

One of the primary jobs of a leader is to create future leaders. You need to be able to identify, develop, and provide guidance and support for those future leaders to reach their full potential.

Your organization's vision should be crystal clear and cascaded to your team, the future leaders, through a well-planned-out strategy. This strategy needs to answer the 'Why do we need to achieve that vision?' question.

What is everyone's role and participation in it, and how will each one, along with yourself, be held publicly accountable for reaching these plans?

In tapping into the capacity of employees, you are helping them reach their full potential, which then translates into reaching your organization's goals, and turning them into future leaders.

Leaders are judged on their team's achievements and outcomes. Therefore, your primary role becomes to get a group of people to work in harmony with each other to deliver superior outcomes.

As a leader, you must always be on the lookout for highly productive people within your team and organization and also outside your organization. You need to be continuously injecting new talent into your team. By adding talented and highly productive individuals to your team, you are raising the bar constantly, and eventually, this will lead to everyone becoming more productive.

When we were young and played football or any other team sports, if we were made captain, we would always pick and choose the best players to be part of our team or try as hard as possible to be part of the best team. We didn't care if we left the weak players standing, waiting to be picked, and we would get upset if we were asked to join a weak team. Why did we fight tooth and nail at that age to get the best player on our team or to join the best team? Simple – because we wanted to win. The winning formula in that case was very simple. The best people equal the best performance, which equals the winning team. Hiring the best people plus eliminating the weak performers equals the best performance, which equals the winning team.

Then why do we choose our colleagues any differently than we chose our teammates when we were young? Who should stay? Who should be developed? Who should be let go of, and who should be made captain? At work, why do we allow our emotions to get the best of us? Why can't we use the same concept? To be a winning team, we need strong players, others who have a burning desire to win, to be recognized, to make a difference. Simply put, if you want to be a winner, you have to be with winners.

WITH POWER COMES RESPONSIBILITY

Learn to identify and track talent. So how do we do that, you say? Fair enough. Start with your own team. Have skip-level meetings with your subordinates.

Where you identify talent, ask your subordinates to delegate extra work to their subordinates, and keep a close eye on their performance. Let them join a couple of your team meetings. Not only will you be developing future leaders but soon everyone in the organization will come to know about this. Even if they are in different departments, they will gravitate towards working with you because they know that they will grow and be successful working in an environment where everyone is given a chance, regardless of their seniority in the organization.

While searching for talent, you need to be aware of the lone wolf, the self-proclaimed hero, the show-off. These individuals go by many names and are very dangerous for the team as they will stop at nothing to look better than the rest, even if it means sabotaging their peers and even their own teammates. As long as they look good and achieve their selfish goals, they do not mind overstepping and cutting down others.

Let's take the football analogy again. The show-off is the footballer who always wants to score and will go to any lengths to keep scoring, even if it means missing most of the shots he takes. He will not pass the ball and allow another person to score. Sooner or later, the rest of the players on the team will stop passing the ball to him. They will reach a stage where they do not mind losing as much as they do not want him to score. In fact, they want him off the team. You, as a leader, should get such individuals off the team until they learn to play as a team member or remove them completely if they do not show any indication that they will change their behavior.

Investing in your people and their development is critical, especially when you want them to lead others. Many times, we have fallen into a pit where we promote the best individual performers and put them in a role that they're not prepared for, causing a vacuum and chaos in both roles. We have lost a wonderful individual, and in their new role, since they have no leadership skills, their weaknesses will reflect on the overall performance of the team.

I remember a time when I promoted a lady. She was the best sales performer in the entire organization with multiple awards for her achievements and was technically very sound. After her promotion, six months later, she came to me and asked if she could get her old job back. I was surprised, but when I took a closer look at her team's performance, I could understand why.

Her team had gone from being in the top five to being the lowest, rock bottom, with multiple problems. She had no skills to lead and was, in fact, getting penalized and losing incentives for not achieving her targets. I still remember her telling me, 'Boss, I was making more money, had more time, less stress, and was happy at my job. Now, I am miserable, and although my salary is higher, it is not even close to the incentives I was making in my earlier role. And to make matters worse, my team as a whole is not making incentives, and they are starting to resign.'

Be careful when promoting a specialist or staff member into a leadership position. This is a very common mistake that I have seen and am guilty of. Just because you have a person who is a subject-matter expert or a star performer who does their job extremely well, that does not mean they can lead a team.

Not only are you losing one of your best star performers but you will be putting the entire team, that the expert will be in charge of, in jeopardy. Double whammy. Great leaders dedicate a lot of time to seeking, identifying, and developing leaders. They seek out people with the greatest leadership potential and invest their time in developing them by working with the best people.

You can build on their strengths and expand your ring of influence rapidly as the organization, and you, are getting the value and influence of all those leaders and the followers. Let's break it down. When you develop one follower, you impact one, and the organization gets the value of one person. When you develop a leader, you are multiplying this effect.

Math Time:

Develop ten followers:

You have the value of ten people and the influence over ten people.

And ten followers multiplied by one equals ten.

- $10 \times 1 = 10$ followers

RINGS OF INFLUENCE

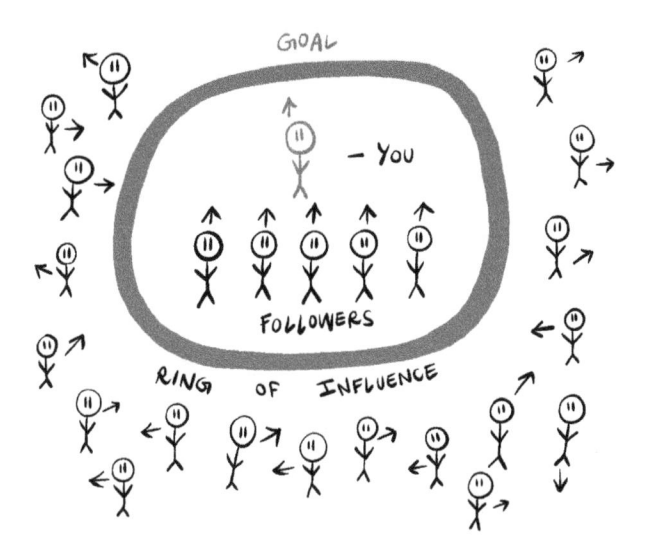

Develop ten leaders:

You have the value of ten people multiplied by all their followers and the influence over these ten leaders and their followers as well.

If these ten leaders each have five followers:

Ten multiplied by five equals fifty.

- 10 x 5 = 50 followers

Simon Sinek, in his book *Leaders Eat Last*, writes, 'It's not how smart the people in the organization are, it's how well they work together. That is the true indicator of future success or the ability to manage through struggle.'

[Diagram: Ring of Influence — an oval containing stick figures labeled "YOU" at top, "LEADERS" in the middle row, and "FOLLOWERS" at the bottom, with arrows pointing up toward "GOAL" above the oval.]

RING OF INFLUENCE

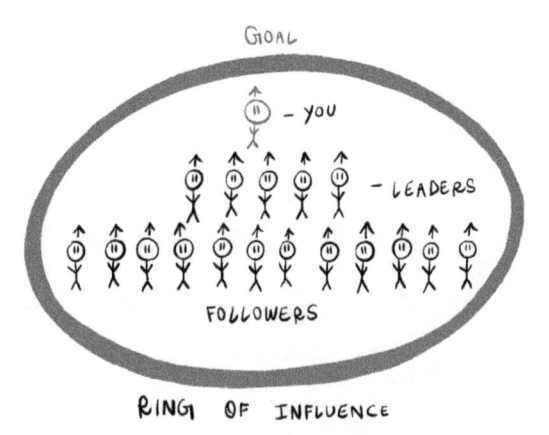

A key part of being a good leader is choosing the right people. It's important to only keep those who are a good fit for your team, and remove those who aren't.

So how do we know if a person is good for the team or not?

By asking yourself these two questions:

1. Knowing what I know today about this person, would I hire them again in the future?
2. If this person resigned today to go to another organization, would I be relieved or upset?

Now you've got your answer. Make a move on it. It's also important to make sure you have the right people on board, and that the most important tasks and projects are appointed to them, not the problems.

As Jim Collins wrote in his book *Good to Great*, 'Successful leaders start by getting the right people on board and removing the wrong ones.' Remember, it's not just about having people on your team. It's about having the right people, with the right strengths.

This will lead us to our next chapter, which looks at how to understand the strengths of your team and how to utilize them.

CHAPTER HIGHLIGHTS

Your philosophy towards future leaders: The creation of future leaders should be your number one duty. You are not there to increase your followers but to increase the leaders that are in your charge. Identify prospects with the capacity to grow into future leaders, invest in their development, and help them reach their full potential.

Be crystal clear: Ensure your organization's vision is clearly understood and communicated to your team and future leaders through a strategic plan. Ensure all are aware of the 'why' behind the vision, clearly define everyone's role and expectations, and establish a fair and tangible public accountability mechanism for achieving the organization's goals.

Raise the bar: Always be on the lookout and inject new talent wherever needed into your team. Surrounding yourself with highly productive individuals will lead to superior performance, creating a culture of growth and excellence.

Identify and track talent: Regularly have skip-level meetings to identify talent within your team and across the organization. Promote the habit of effective delegation to test and develop future leaders. Mainly make sure that everyone is given a chance to grow, regardless of seniority and environment, and provide an opportunity for everyone to strive and shine.

Beware of the lone wolf: Avoid, at all costs, individuals who prioritize personal glory over teamwork. Remove them, as they will eventually sabotage others for their own personal benefit. Foster a culture of success through collaboration.

Choose the right people: One of your main strengths should be the choices you make when putting your team together. Never think of names. Instead, think of the role that needs filling first, then think about who is the perfect fit for that role.

Be extremely cautious when promoting specialists or star performers into leadership positions. Make sure that the leadership skills that you are looking for have been cultivated and the willingness to become a future leader has been demonstrated. Investing time in developing future leaders is crucial for the success of everyone – yourself, the individual, the organization, and your customers – but choosing the wrong people will have an adverse effect on all. Contemplate this for a while – as important as it is to have the right team members promoted and hired, the importance is amplified when it comes to the removal of individuals who do not align with the team's values or do not contribute effectively.

Know your people's strengths: Utilize the strengths of your team members, and align individual tasks and projects based on individual strengths. The understanding and utilization of their strengths will lead to improved confidence within the team and will affect overall performance.

In summary, the development of future leaders is not just your duty as a leader. It is a strategic imperative for any successful leader. A noble deed indeed.

By identifying and developing talent that fosters teamwork and understanding individual strengths, you will be able to use these strengths to create and expand a solid ring of influence for yourself that will help you achieve exceptional outcomes.

Embrace this sophisticated ideology of developing leaders, and you will transform yourself into a leader who creates a threshold for perfection.

CHAPTER 11

MASTERING TEAM STRENGTHS

You Are Only As Strong As Your Weakest Link

> *'Successful careers are not planned. They develop when people are prepared for opportunities because they know their strengths.'*
>
> – PETER F. DRUCKER

Leaders are responsible for realizing the value of building on the strengths of staff. There's a tendency in most organizations to focus on weaknesses and try to create change. However, focusing on strengths is a quicker, more efficient way to reach higher performance. Focus on a few major areas where superior performance will result in excellent output, set priorities, and stay the course.

By the end of this chapter, you will realize that strengths are key to positive growth in an organization and for building the right team spirit.

The graphs below illustrate how working on one of your team member's strengths rather than their weaknesses results in accelerated growth in performance levels, and what this could mean for mastering your leadership craft.

View these graphs:

Fig A shows your current strengths and weaknesses.

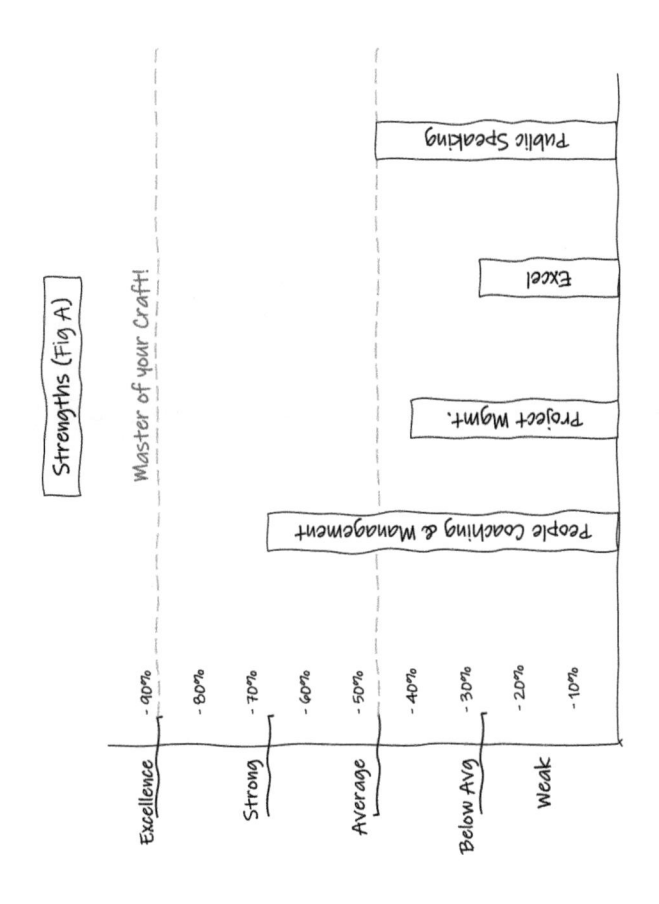

Strengths (Fig A)

- Public Speaking: 20%
- Excel: 30%
- Project Mgmt.: 40%
- People Coaching & Management: 50%

Scale:
- Excellence: 90%
- Strong: 70–80%
- Average: 50–60%
- Below Avg: 30–40%
- Weak: 10–20%

Master of your Craft!

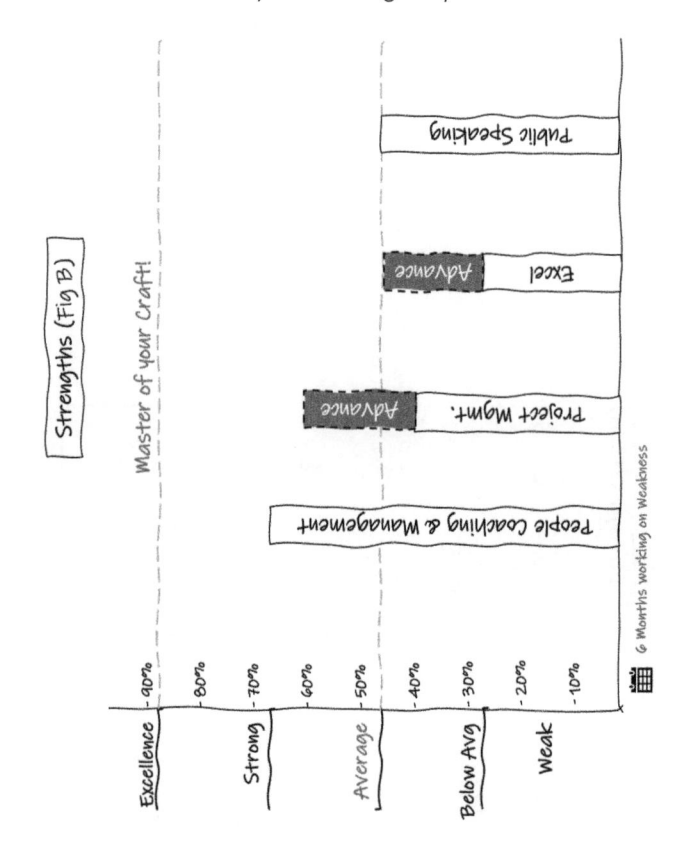

Fig B shows six months of you working on your weakness.

Strengths (Fig B)

Master of your Craft!

- Public Speaking — 10% (Weak)
- Excel — 30% (Below Avg) + Advance
- Project Mgmt. — 50% (Average) + Advance
- People Coaching & Management — 60% (between Average and Strong)

Scale:
- Excellence — 90%
- Strong — 80%
- (70%)
- (60%)
- Average — 50%
- Below Avg — 40%
- (30%)
- (20%)
- Weak — 10%

6 Months working on Weakness

Fig C shows six months of you working on your strengths.

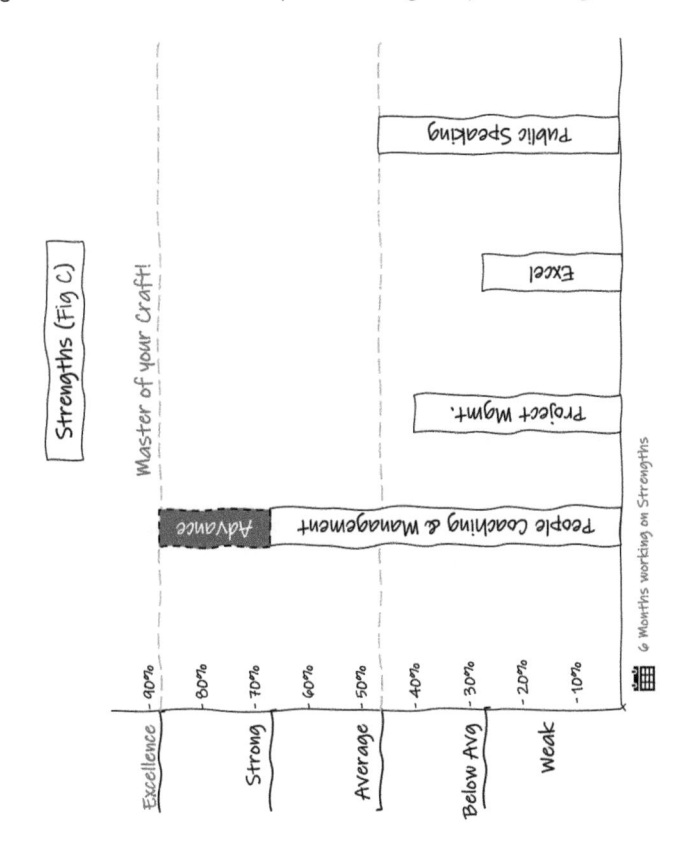

Strengths (Fig C)

Skill	Level
People Coaching & Management	Advance (toward Strong)
Project Mgmt.	~30% (Below Avg/Weak)
Excel	~30% (Below Avg)
Public Speaking	~25% (Weak)

Scale: Excellence 90% / Strong 80-70% / Average 60-50% / Below Avg 40-30% / Weak 20-10%

Master of your Craft

6 Months working on Strengths

FOCUS ON STRENGTHS

Position yourself where your strengths can translate into results and where they can add value for your organization, your followers, and yourself.

Moving from average to strong is far more time-consuming and harder than getting from strong to excellent. Yet we spend countless hours focusing on the weaknesses of our subordinates and ourselves, trying to make below-average performers into average.

Instead, you should be making an average performer focus on their strengths and make them into a star performer. We can perform and excel only from our strengths. We cannot reach great heights through our weaknesses. Trying to accomplish greatness through weakness is a losing battle. In order to become great achievers, we need to know and grow our strengths.

As a strong leader, you should not only be aware of your strengths but also aware of the core strengths of each of your direct reports, and if they are in the relevant job or have the relevant projects and tasks, where they are utilizing at least eighty percent of their strengths.

Team Strength & utilization

Direct Report	Known Strengths	Role	80% Used in current Role	Remarks
Amira	Staff Discipline	Head of Branches	Yes	Experienced in managing large staff count at multiple locations
Mariam	Stakeholder Mgmt.	Head of Product	Yes	Alignment with internal and external stakeholders
Ahmed	Operations	Head of Operations	Yes	Process re-engineering expert (multiple gaps in processes)
Mansour	Selling	Head of Sales	Yes	Managing large teams through incentives
Hind	Projects & Tech.	Head of Complaints	No	Lacks an eye for detail and customer empathy
Hassan	New, Small Team mgmt.	Head of Call Center	No	Lacks experience in service levels and work force management
Khalid	Great work ethic	Head of Quality Assurance	Yes	Black belt in Six Sigma, has over 20 years of experience in QA
Rashid	New, Recently Appointed	Head of Key Clients	No	Lacks experience and relationship management skills

Based on the above/previous grid fill-in the below one for your team

Team Strength & utilization

Direct Report	Known Strengths	Role	80% Used in current Role	Remarks

Ask yourself, using the grid, what is each person in your team known for?

What is it you want to be known for?

If someone had to describe you, what would they say?

You are extremely good at...

A strong leader knows how to best utilize his or her team's strengths and will always do their best to hire staff that are strong in the areas where the leader is weak. No one is strong in all areas.

OPTIMIZING LEADERSHIP STRENGTHS

Not everyone is fully aware of their strengths. People are not aware of their latent abilities or what they really could and should bring to the table. It is like a blind spot, and since they are not aware, they are not in a position to consciously utilize their strong points. By identifying the strengths of each individual in your team and letting them know what you have uncovered within them, you will be raising their awareness and confidence.

Tip: Once you reveal to your subordinates what their true strengths are, ask them this.

'Now that you know what your strength is and what you want to be known for, how can you use this strength best to its full potential to take the team and the organization forward?'

Let's start learning how to identify team strengths.

In your corporate journey, you will get promoted many times, or move into different roles, or maybe even different companies and industries. So how do you go about meeting your new team?

First, arrange a one-on-one meeting with each team member, just for a casual chat. Once that is done, call all of them together. At your first meeting, your opening statement should be, 'I respect a person who challenges me and the team, as only when we challenge each other can we learn best practices and utilize all the collective experiences that we have in this room. Now, let's do a quick exercise to demonstrate what I mean by all the experience in this room. Let us see how experienced we are collectively.'

Make a list on a whiteboard or a flipchart, and follow the examples provided below:

Name:	**Years of Experience:**
Amira	19
Mariam	15
Hind	12
Mansour	22
Ahmed (self)	21
Hamda	20
Rashid	17
Total:	**126 years**

'So collectively, we have 126 years of experience, which means, together, we can move mountains for this organization if we all have the same goal. When all our agendas are aligned, we have healthy conflict and do not sugarcoat critical information, which means we are able to have constructive conversations. Do not think that you might be pointing fingers at the person sitting next to you. That is not what we are here to do. We are not pointing fingers. We are identifying bottlenecks, and only by first identifying them can we come up with a solution and execute it.'

This is a tough-love stance, but it is best to be transparent rather than create an illusion of reality. People don't like to be judged; therefore, focusing on strengths rather than weaknesses will provide a guide for the team to take ownership of their actions and feel supported in discovering and rectifying their flaws. Being open, with clear lines of communication, will create a teamwork attitude and everyone will be motivated to achieve the common goal for the success of the organization.

GREAT LEADERS BUILD GREAT TEAMS

Once you have uncovered the strengths of your team members, look for opportunities and roles that demand these strengths and place them there. Once you have put them in a role where they can fully utilize their strengths, shine a spotlight on them. Make others aware of what they are doing and of their progress. This will boost their confidence, uplift their morale, and encourage their efforts. The team members who are functioning at optimum levels will be noticed, and this will get others wanting to work for you.

Why should others want to work for you?

They are aware of your capacity to develop leadership qualities in them. They too want to learn, grow, be listened to, be part of your A-team, be successful, and be developed into future leaders.

After all, true leaders develop leaders, and that's exactly what you are capable of achieving.

What is your added benefit of shining the spotlight? You will get an influx of people who will want to join your team, and you will have the luxury to cherry-pick the best of the best, or the ones with the highest potential for development.

Creating success for others at work is like gravity. The more powerful and influential you become, the more you will pull everyone towards you. Your influence over them will be in abundance, even before you start to lead them, as you now have a track record.

You will be recognized as the 'maker of leaders.'
If leadership means having influence over someone, you cannot get more influential than guiding and developing your followers, who, in turn, develop followers into future leaders.

John C. Maxwell, in his book *5 Levels of Leadership*, writes, 'As a rule of thumb, try to hire and position people in such a way that 80% of the time they work in their strength zone, 15% of the time they work in the learning zone, 5% of the time they work outside their strength zone, and 0% of the time they work in their weakness zone.'

CHAPTER HIGHLIGHTS

Strengths: Take the time to find out and reflect on your own strengths, and at the same time, each team member's strengths. Understand how they and you can contribute to your personal and professional growth and become capable of taking the organization to new heights.

Work from and on strengths: Stop trying to fix weaknesses. Focus on nurturing and developing strengths. Make sure your team members spend the majority of their time working in their strength zone, where they can excel, achieve excellence, and develop their own leadership skills.

Provide opportunities for growth: Identifying your team's strengths is the beginning. Now make sure you place them in roles or give them tasks that allow them to fully utilize their identified areas of strength. Provide equal opportunities for all who are willing to put in the hard work for continuous learning and growth in their strength zones. Celebrate the wins, achievements, and progress of your team members. Acknowledge their efforts no matter how big or small. Let everyone know what strength each team member is known for – make it public. Never shy away from an opportunity to boost their confidence and motivate them to strive for excellence.

Delegate wisely: Always consider the individual team member's strengths before allocating responsibilities. Delegate tasks to them that align with their strengths to maximize productivity and job satisfaction. Set them up for excellence, not for a fall.

Develop future leaders: Real leaders develop future leaders. Focus more on mentoring and developing the strengths and hidden talent of your team members rather than spending countless hours on their weaknesses and achieving mediocre results.

By creating future leaders through mastering team strengths and leveraging individual talents, you can create your 'A-team' – a high-performing team that propels your organization towards excellence and success.

CHAPTER 12
ENVIRONMENT

Motivational Approaches In An Organization

You have heard the widely used word 'motivation.' Yet how one can motivate others remains unclear. In essence, motivation is the impulse to repeat behaviors that build a momentum of action-oriented outcomes, despite the amount of work involved.

As a leader, you hold the power to create an environment where people feel good, not stressed, and become self-motivated individuals. To achieve this, first, it is essential to establish clear expectations and have fair differentiation between high and low performers.

By the end of this chapter, you will understand how important the right environment influences the behavior of the employees, and how leaders are responsible for creating the right environment through differentiation.

When people witness the positive effects of hard work and dedication, it gives them a deep sense of satisfaction and drives them to strive for even greater achievements. As human beings, we crave tangible evidence that our work efforts are appreciated, that our dedication is paying off and that our work is worthwhile. We want to be known for our services and for others to see and acknowledge them. This type of environment, where staff are encouraged to make a meaningful difference, becomes a self-motivating culture that propels people towards success.

ENGAGE YOUR TEAM

Engage your team by setting clear expectations with regular follow-ups and reviews. When you provide the necessary resources for success and a clear target while holding people accountable for their commitments, over time, the high-stretch expectations become part of your team's DNA. This drives a culture where people hold themselves and others accountable, often to higher standards.

Tip: Do not stretch so much that the team breaks. Think of stretching a rubber band. You can stretch it only so much before it breaks. Imagine keeping a rubber band in the freezer for a couple of days and then one fine morning taking it out and pulling on it. It will break without stretching to its full potential.

This is the same with a team that has had mediocre expectations placed on them in the past and suddenly gets high expectations. They will panic. They will break!

Increase the expectations gradually, making sure you raise the bar every time a milestone has been achieved.

Another way to do this is by linking rewards to performance and making performance easily measurable. How many times have you not known why or how the incentives or bonuses were paid out? Making it easily measurable drives the change that an organization wants. You need to define what gets appreciated, what gets rewarded, and what ultimately leads to a promotion. This needs to be defined very, very clearly. You must make sure that there is a clear difference made in terms of all of the above, between the performers and the non-performers. As Lawrence Bossidy asserts in his book *Execution*, 'Open differentiation is the mother's milk of building a performance culture.'

To ensure that people produce the specific results you desire, it is important to reward them accordingly. The culture you want to establish needs to be linked to the reward system. This seems like common sense, but surprisingly, many leaders and corporations don't implement performance rewards that correlate to the behavior or culture that they want to drive. Companies that usually do not perform well often don't make execution and output leading factors when an individual needs to be rewarded or promoted.

There is not enough differentiation in incentives between top-performing individuals and those who are not. When distinctions are made in a clear, measurable way, they become ingrained in the company's way of life. As a leader, it is important to emphasize these distinctions and let people know that they are not being promoted and compensated for seniority, but for their caliber and output.

Do a survey.

Feedback Survey

	Strongly Disagree	Disagree	Neutral	Agree	Strongly Agree	Comments
1. Communication and Feedback: How effectively does your manager communicate with you, providing clear expectations and regular feedback on your work?	○	○	○	○	○	Comments go here
2. Support and Development: Does your manager actively support your professional development and growth within the company?	○	○	○	○	○	Comments go here
3. Recognition and Appreciation: Does your manager recognize and appreciate your contributions and efforts?	○	○	○	○	○	Comments go here
4. Leadership and Decision-Making: How would you rate your manager's leadership skills, including their ability to make informed decisions and lead by example?	○	○	○	○	○	Comments go here
5. Work-Life Balance: Does your manager respect your work-life balance and make reasonable efforts to ensure you have a healthy work-life equilibrium?	○	○	○	○	○	Comments go here

Send it across or do it through a system to maintain anonymity. Keep it confidential to ensure it is a survey that people will fill out.

I have provided the template for a survey that could be sent to your staff to understand what type of rewards, differentiation, and distinctions they desire or require, which leads us to our next chapter, which looks at accountability and ownership.

CHAPTER HIGHLIGHTS

Get ready to create a highly motivated and engaged team by taking charge as a leader and implementing motivational approaches in your organization today. Foster a culture of self-motivation and recognition, and drive your team towards greater achievements and success.

Clear expectations: There is nothing like clarity and realistic expectations. Ensure everyone recognizes their roles and responsibilities, as well as the objectives they need to achieve. Top performers have to be differentiated and rewarded based on their performance in a very fair, tangible, and measurable way. Create a culture where excellence is appreciated and rewarded.

Accountability: Hold yourself and your team members accountable for your department's commitments, but first make sure that your team has the right tools and resources to deliver the commitments.

Engagement surveys: Conduct regular engagement surveys to gather feedback from your team. Use the insights to tailor your motivational strategies, rewards, and recognition programs – learn what is best for the people, from the people.

Culture that values results: Make sure everyone knows that you will pick performance over seniority any day, and communicate that promotions and rewards are based on performance and output. It does not matter how long you have been in the organization. What matters is what have you done and are doing for the organization.

Continuous improvement: Continuously review and refine your approaches. Be open to feedback and adapt your strategies to inspire and meet the ever-evolving needs of your team.

By implementing these tactics and fostering a positive, motivating environment, you can inspire your team to reach new heights of performance and create a culture of self-motivated individuals who are driven to achieve success.

Remember, as a leader, your actions and decisions play a significant role in shaping the motivational climate within your organization. Start making a difference today!

CHAPTER 13

ENHANCING CONNECTIONS

Change, Communication, Trust

'If you do not change, you will fall behind the changing times. If you do not develop, you will miss your ride on the world's express train. And if you do not gain knowledge, you will go backwards as days move forward.'

– HIS HIGHNESS SHEIKH MOHAMMED BIN RASHID AL MAKTOUM, VICE PRESIDENT AND PRIME MINISTER OF THE UNITED ARAB EMIRATES

If we are not open to change, we will not be able to progress. The only thing permanent in life is change.

By the end of this chapter, you will learn how leaders can enhance their capabilities with a trio of skills, enabling teams to adapt to change through communication and building trust.

Resistance to change is a common occurrence and manifests itself in various ways. The key factor that triggers this resistance is often a lack of understanding of the benefits of the proposed change.

Attitudes towards change differ from individual to individual depending on the level of involvement and understanding of the change and its benefits. For change to be effective, it requires active participation by employees, as this increases their sense of ownership towards the proposed changes. Such participation enables employees to view things from different perspectives and fosters a greater understanding of the vision behind proposed changes.

Employees tend to be more receptive to a vision when they fully comprehend it. At the core of the issue is uncertainty. People want to stay in their comfort zone and do things that they are familiar with. People who are involved and understand the change usually accept it.

To make sure people accept change, you, as a leader, must make sure you continuously communicate with all your people why this change is necessary and how it will be successfully implemented. You also need to communicate the drawbacks of things staying the same. At the same time, ask all the staff for their input and help to bring about this change. You'll be surprised at how quickly staff are willing to change and help you deliver the change needed, as long as they fully understand the reasoning behind it and have been asked to pitch in.

Change is an inescapable part of our lives and represents new opportunities for organizations and people who are willing to learn and adapt. Without the ability to embrace change, think creatively, and adapt accordingly, human beings would still be living in caves. It is this innate desire for change that has led to human progress.

Individuals and organizations who shut themselves off from the outside world and believe that they already have all the specialized knowledge about their field are putting a lid on their own growth. Unfortunately, they remain stagnant in a world that is constantly evolving.

To further elaborate on the above, let's take a look at Kodak, a company that went from market dominance to bankruptcy.

A LEADER'S LEGACY

THE RISE AND FALL OF EASTMAN KODAK

Eastman Kodak is an iconic American brand. The company was established at the end of the nineteenth century. Kodak revolutionized the photography industry by giving every consumer the ability to develop their own personal pictures, at a low cost. However, Kodak stubbornly continued to embrace film photography long after consumers had shifted to digital-based photography, and this led Kodak to declare bankruptcy in 2012.

In 1880, George Eastman created the first photographic dry plates to be used in the mass development of photographs.

In 1892, Eastman incorporated the Eastman Kodak Company, which focused on several diverse activities related to the photographic industry, including photographic-based chemicals, materials, and film.

Through this extensive diversification of its products, Kodak became the dominant player in the photography industry globally. At its peak, Kodak controlled eighty percent of the market share of the photographic film industry.

DIGITAL PHOTOGRAPHY: THE BEGINNING OF THE END

Since all the Kodak executives had a background in running a film-based company, they did not understand that digital photography would be the ultimate disruptive innovation in the industry. By being film-centric, Kodak ignored the warning signs that photography would change forever with the adoption of digital software. Not only was this type of photography more convenient but it was also cheaper. Customers had slipped away to digital photography while Kodak continued with film-based photography.

In addition, digital photography allowed for the easy transfer of images electronically from one source to another. With the explosion of social media, users demanded instant access to pictures, and it became commonplace for pictures to be posted immediately after being taken.

There was resistance to change, and Kodak continued to focus on its film business. The famous Kodachrome film, which used to be the ultimate standard for both amateur and professional photographers, was not discontinued until 2006, long after consumers had already shifted to digital images.

Kodak was unable to adapt to the changing competitive landscape in the photography industry. This resulted in negative cash flows and forced Kodak to abandon any new investments in film technology by 2003.

In January 2012, when Eastman Kodak filed for Chapter 11 bankruptcy, after 131 years of being in business, the investors were not surprised.

Kodak's revenue in 1990 was $19 billion and dropped to $2 billion by 2015. At its peak, Kodak employed 145,000 people but this number dropped drastically to 8,000 by 2015.

By ignoring the warning signs from fierce competitors and the adoption of digital photography, Kodak was left behind as other companies developed a more synergistic link with the needs of customers. The fall of the giant was due to ignoring the ever-evolving environment and not embracing change.

The success or failure of any business organization rests on its ability to evolve and embrace change, and the same applies to human beings' growth and development. The way a leader drives change and adaptation among teams will have the most significant impact on success or failure.

COMMUNICATION TRANSPARENCY

Good communication means simplicity in speaking, actively listening, understanding the other person's perspective, and holding back criticism. Good communication is based on logic, sound reasoning, and a will to connect. Many a time when we have our meetings with the IT department or technical departments, we hear tech jargon like 'UI' and 'UX,' leaving many unsure and confused.

Not everyone is an IT, finance, or HR expert. The use of jargon to a wider audience beyond specialists usually has an adverse effect. Instead of clarifying, it confuses and creates misunderstandings. Not everyone understands the words being used, and most people feel that if they ask, they will look bad in front of their peers and colleagues.

As a leader, active listening is another critical skill that needs to be mastered. It involves giving full attention to peers, subordinates, or anyone that you might come in contact with, just in the same way you would give your attention to your boss.

Good listening is a highly active process and a main component of clear communication. To be a good listener, you should think before you speak, and listen with respect. Sometimes, it can be challenging to listen actively, especially during a heated discussion or when you are upset about what you are hearing.

However, as the old saying goes, we have two ears and one mouth for a reason. We have two ears and one mouth so we can listen twice as much as we speak.

When we are angry, upset, confused, or surprised, there will be unnecessary words spoken, words that hurt or lead to upset people. Keeping silent is an active choice and requires great discipline.

By mastering active listening, you become a more effective leader and improve your communication skills dramatically. Remember, what you say is a reflection of how well you have listened. They are two sides of the same coin.

Understanding the other person's perspective is as important as active listening. When trying to solve the problem – be it for a peer, subordinate, sibling, or child – never rush into fixing things, and never undermine the person with the problem.

First, make sure that both of you are sitting on the same side of the table and looking at the matter at hand through the same set of lenses.

Here, you listen twice as much as you talk and truly try to understand the other person's perspective without thinking about yourself. Many times, when somebody tells us what's happening with them and with their lives, be it a problem or an issue they have, we fall into the trap of straightaway jumping on the wagon and starting to speak about our own similar problems. This is not the time to speak about ourselves; it's the time to listen to the other person.

What do you see above? The number 6. However, flip the book upside down and you will see the number 9 or the letter g. Never be in a rush to prescribe an antidote before making sure your diagnosis is accurate. Also, avoid giving unsolicited opinions or advice.

While communicating as a leader, giving constructive feedback, both good and bad, is one of the key responsibilities. Besides that, the leader must set clear written expectations for the staff to identify the skills needed and help them aim with precision so that they are able to hit the right targets.

This should be done on a one-to-one basis at least once a month so that there are no surprises at the end of the year or at the time of the evaluation. Not only is this the employee's right, but it makes them better at their jobs, which results in higher productivity. However, the manner in which we give feedback makes all the difference. We need to remember it is a two-way discussion to improve your staff's values, productivity, motivation, skills, and morale.

There is a thin line between productive feedback and criticism. Although both are feedback, they stand at two ends of the spectrum. When we criticize, we set the other person beneath us, in an inferior position, which hurts their sense of pride. This then pushes them into a defensive position and forces them to justify their actions. This makes them feel worse than before the meeting started, which is exactly the opposite of what is intended by having the meeting.

You have definitely heard the word 'coaching,' so what is coaching?

When at work, and we hear Ahmed and Hind need coaching, we, by default, assume that Ahmed and Hind are about to get punished. That is what Ahmed and Hind and most of your subordinates will think as well. So why is that?

Simply put, most managers only coach when the person has done something wrong or as part of the disciplinary action process to issue warnings. But the real reason coaching exists is to develop those who are reporting directly to you, making them future leaders and helping them reach their fullest potential.

The most efficient way to coach is to observe the person in action and then provide specific constructive feedback that points to examples of behavior and performance that are good, that need to be developed, and that need to be changed.

During a coaching session, you can:

- Share your experiences to inspire the team.
- Point out any blind spots that your team member has.
- Find out what your team member's strengths are.
- Find out the areas of development needed.
- Agree upon clear expectations.
- Find out how well your team member is performing against expectations.
- Discuss what needs to be delivered and how.
- Outline the tools, resources, and support that the team needs to deliver in accordance with expectations.
- Identify where they stand currently and where they will be by the end of the year if they continue along this path.

Coaching is a wonderful tool that, if used in the right way, makes sure your staff members receive all the support and development they need to grow and become future dependable leaders. Regular coaching sessions have proven to improve the performance of employees, since this enables them to be clear on where they stand and where they are supposed to be headed, and they can receive guidance upfront if they need to change direction to achieve a better outcome.

Yet, sadly, what happens in most organizations is that managers only have one-to-one meetings with their team members twice a year – once for the mid-year rating and once for the year-end rating. I have seen managers do only one meeting at year end, and sadly, I have also seen managers who do no meetings and then give a rating to the employee while saying, 'This is your rating as per the management'!

What a disastrous way to manage, develop, and lead…

Do you think it is fair to rate someone you have not tried to develop?

Coaching is not only a tool to develop your team, it is also to ensure that you, as a leader, can identify and understand all the needs of your subordinates and build your **A-team.**

Below, I have provided a coaching template, which can be modified as needed:

Employee Coaching Template

Employee Name: Lamya
Coaching Date: 21/06/23
Title / Position: VP – digital marketing
Supervisor: Ahmed

COACHING TOPIC / AREA
Communicating with the team
Lamya has encountered challenges in effectively communicating and maintaining the team's awareness of her task progress. This has led to a limited visibility and challenges in distributing workloads.

DESIRED OUTCOMES *(List desired behaviors, knowledge, skills, etc.)*
Develop friendly relationships with people
Enhance your presence and strengthen connections.
Increase transparency regarding Lamya's ongoing tasks.

BENEFITS OF CHANGE *(How will employee actions or performance be positively impacted)*
Lamya will be comfortable sharing with team, increasing productivity and efficiency
Lamya will be actively engaged and content in her role.
This will lead to an enhanced team dynamic and an improved office culture.

ACTION PLAN *(What actions can be taken to achieve these goals)*
Utilize group MS teams channel to maintain connectivity within the team.
Establish a collaborative status update document or utilize a Microsoft Planner board.
Provide training on office communication norms and best practices.

TIMELINE *(Write out a timeline for the plan and when to follow up)*
After two weeks, conduct a follow-up to gauge the progress of the team updates.
One month following Lamya's training session, evaluate her communication skills and overall skill enhancement.

Here are some questions and tips that are helpful when creating your tailor-made coaching log.

- State the expected outcome very clearly.
- Agree upon the methods of meeting the expected outcomes.
- Always ask as a coach: What support do you need? What support can I extend to you to ensure you have all the right resources and tools to deliver your agreed outcomes?
- What is one thing I currently do that you want me to continue doing?
- What is one thing I do that you want me to stop doing and why? How is it affecting you?
- What can I do to make you more productive?

TRUST

The more trust you have in your relationship, the easier and faster things get done. The higher the trust level, the safer you both feel. 'Simply put, trust means confidence,' says Stephen M. R. Covey.

When we hear the word 'trust,' usually our emotional side comes into play. Values, integrity, dependencies, intent, motives, understanding – all these things connect to human emotions; however, that is just fifty percent of the equation of what is known as one's character.

There is another side that is usually left out but is just as important as character, if not more so, depending on the circumstances at hand.

Competence, capabilities, and skills.

For you to understand this better, I would like to share an exercise I did for fifty managers within my team. On a whiteboard, I wrote a little bit about myself and a brief bio: '*I have over two decades of leadership experience. I have led and managed over 3000 individuals over the span of my career and guided over 100 individuals and helped them grow in their careers.*' After that, I asked a question: 'How many of you would trust me to be your mentor and develop your leadership skills?' Everyone was eager and put their hands up.

Then, I started writing a bit more about myself: '*I hate to fly. I usually get airsick on flights. I am afraid of heights. I cannot get my bearings straight when it comes to navigation, even if my life depends on it.*' Then I asked the second question: 'How many of you are willing to take a helicopter ride with me as the pilot?'

How many do you think raised their hands? **Zero.**

So why is that? Do you think that they do not trust me or my character? No, they do. They very much trust me and my character. What they do not trust is my capability as a pilot.

As a leader, you need to know each team member's capabilities. It is okay to tell them, 'I do not trust you can deliver this particular task, not because of your willingness or your character, but because of your capabilities.' This way, you let them know the truth without creating any tension in your relationship and will be able to give the task to someone else capable without emotions attached. You do not doubt this person's character; you doubt their capabilities. You do not have confidence in the person's capabilities. It's nothing to do with their character. Hence, **Character + Capabilities = Trust**.

Trust is related to much more than just character.

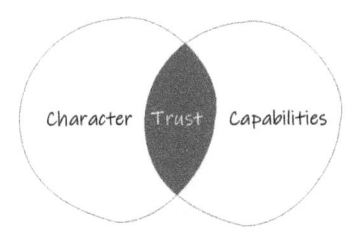

(Venn diagram: Character ∩ Capabilities = Trust)

Ask yourself or your organization about this aspect of leadership and reflect on it. Which of these three are your weakest links, and how are you going to put in place a plan to strengthen them? At the same time, think about which of the key players in your team have these characteristics and capabilities, and how you are going to develop them as well.

CHAPTER HIGHLIGHTS

Embrace change: Change is inevitable, and recognition of this is essential for progress. As a leader, embrace change. Encourage your teams to be adaptable and view change as an opportunity.

Advocate effective communication: Encourage clear and simple communication. Avoid technical jargon, especially when communicating with non-specialists. Master the art of active listening and seek to understand the perspectives of others.

Become a master at coaching: Use coaching as a tool to develop your team members and help them reach their full potential. Identify their needs with regular coaching sessions and lead them to higher productivity and better performance.

Understand the characteristics of trust: Trust is a combination of character and capabilities. Assess each team member's capabilities and provide support to enhance their strengths to boost their skills and confidence.

By embracing change, practicing effective communication, and building trust through coaching and support, you will be enhancing the capabilities of your team, and this will foster a positive and productive work environment.

CHAPTER 14
PLANNING AND OWNERSHIP

Taking Accountability

They say failing to plan is planning to fail, but what comes after a great plan?

EXECUTION

A great plan alone, without proper execution, is pie in the sky, an idea at most. To execute this plan, the key ingredients required are accountability and ownership. Planning is just one aspect of leading a team.

As a leader, you need to have the ability to encourage your team to take ownership of the plan. You will need to hold, first, yourself accountable and then your team by being firm but fair. To translate the plan into superior results and services on behalf of your customers, you need to have the right people involved, not after the planning is done, with a top-down approach, but at the initial stages of planning.

The involvement of staff needs to be well structured. The individuals who will be executing the plan and those who are subject matter experts in the processes need to be involved. By including them in the planning stages, this becomes their plan, which translates to self-accountability and ownership.

No one wants to see their plans undelivered. As a leader, building a team that collaborates and works very closely together to deliver superior results is your responsibility. This also means lifting the morale of staff. Getting them involved will have the following impact on these individuals:

1. They will feel needed.
2. They will feel heard.
3. They will have the opportunity to understand the bigger picture.
4. They will have the opportunity to influence how it operates.
5. They will be able to learn from each other.
6. They will be able to showcase any hidden talents.
7. They will feel important and part of the future growth of the organization.

As the leader, the sole person responsible for the success or failure of your team is you. You cannot blame your subordinates for not delivering or not being up to the mark. If a subordinate is underperforming, it is your job to find out why, coach them, support them, train them, and provide them with all the necessary tools they need to succeed while making sure they have the right skill sets required to perform their current role. If they don't, it is your responsibility to move them to another team or department.

If they fail, then you have to let them go so that the rest of the team is not pulled down by one person. To keep an underperformer is unfair to the rest of the organization and yourself.

Good performers want to be held accountable as they feel that they have been given the opportunity to do something valuable, and they know that their boss trusts them. They actually thrive in an environment where they know that everyone will be rewarded and held accountable for their deliverables. They also know that poor performers won't just slip by.

Such fair accountability builds extraordinary trust, especially since it makes people feel secure with the knowledge that everyone will be held accountable to certain standards. Not holding people accountable, on the other hand, specifically the non-performers and the slackers, has an adverse effect, not only on the bad performers but on the good performers as well. In fact, it has a domino effect by creating disappointment, inequality, and insecurity – people just feel they have been treated unfairly.

UNDERPERFORMERS AFFECT THE ENTIRE TEAM

To further elaborate on this, let's look a bit more closely at a common situation. Let's imagine you have two direct reports, Mansour and Khalifa. At the end of the year, you rate both of them as outstanding or strong.

Mansour never misses a day's work. He is always there, and you can depend on him. He delivered the financial numbers and behaved as expected while achieving all of his KPIs and objectives.

On the other side, you have Khalifa who came to work late multiple times and has used up all his sick leave. You know for a fact that he is not sick or suffering from any illness. He has an attitude problem with his peers and is behind on his KPIs and objectives, yet both are rated the same.

Don't tell me you have never come across this.

Unfortunately, I have seen this happen many, many times over the years. At year end, managers do not want to have that tough talk because they have not coached the staff throughout the year. The easiest way for the manager to get out of this tight spot is to give an okay-to-good rating to all the staff.

And this leads to Mansour feeling cheated. He wonders, 'What's the point in giving my best? I will always be rated the same way.' Demoralized and feeling defeated, Mansour's performance starts to drop. While Khalifa starts feeling that he has beaten the system and starts to spread rumors of how to get away scot-free while doing the minimum. Khalifa tells the ones he's in close contact with that they are dummies for working hard. After all, bad employees want others to be bad as well. Birds of a feather...

What do you think is going to happen in such a culture where people are rated unfairly? People will start to get demoralized and team performance will drop. If we know all of this, then why do we still see managers treating staff and rating staff unfairly?

The top reasons for unfair ratings are:

1. Nepotism and favoritism.
2. Managers don't want to deal with difficult employees.
3. There is no proper rating system or process where collaboration takes place. It is an open discussion with all managers and peers regarding staff ratings collectively.
4. There is no monthly or quarterly coaching to support year-end decisions.

In a worse scenario, the manager rates people poorly and tells them it is on the instructions of the managers. And there is even the excuse that it is HR that forced their ratings down.

Have you ever heard this response? 'We have a bell curve to maintain. It is not personal. You just got caught in the crossfire.' Of course, it is personal! It is a person's full year of work that is being rated, and if the manager cannot or does not have the necessary skills to have tough but fair conversations, then they should not be managing people in the first place.

The grid shows how the staff behaviour is affected when the accountability is fair or unfair

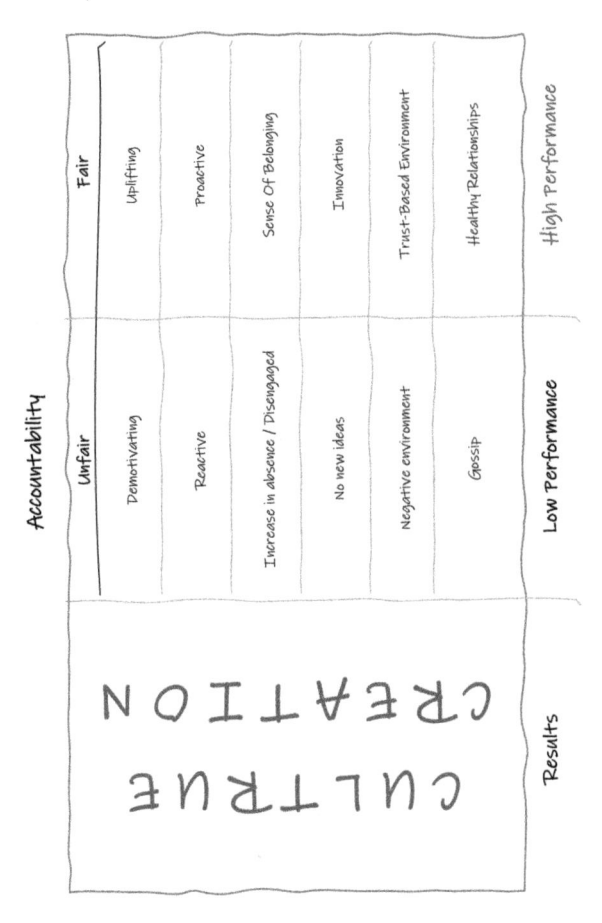

Accountability							
Fair	Uplifting	Proactive	Sense Of Belonging	Innovation	Trust-Based Environment	Healthy Relationships	High Performance
Unfair	Demotivating	Reactive	Increase in absence / Disengaged	No new ideas	Negative environment	Gossip	Low Performance

CULTURE CREATION — Results

PLANNING

Imagine that you are a star chef, a master of your craft, and are asked to prepare your best meal ever. Before you start, you need to plan and make sure you have all the tools and ingredients to cook this delicious meal. So, you first need to know what you're going to cook. Then you make sure you have all the tools – pots, pans, ovens, a fryer... and then all the ingredients – the meat, bread, rice, water... Now start mixing and cooking, one step after the other in a particular fashion and format until your three-hat Michelin meal is ready and *bon appétit*.

It is the same with any project or task that we are planning to deliver in life.

Steps for planning:

1. Know what you want to achieve or where you want to be.
2. Where are you now?
3. What will be delivered?
4. What are the necessary tools, ingredients, and resources needed to deliver?
5. What is the order of the steps?
6. How long will it take?
7. Execute.

Before carving your plans in stone, it is critical to have your team's buy-in. And how do you achieve this? By making them part of the planning. Not only will they be fully committed, but you might be surprised with the new learnings and ideas. When you make them part of the planning, you will have a better chance of success as this is their baby as well, and no one wants to see their baby fail.

PLANNING AND OWNERSHIP

THE OWNERSHIP PROCESS

Let me share with you a small story of twenty-one babies, and an outcome of ownership.

At one point in time, I had forty senior managers reporting directly to me, and we were in the middle of COVID. Those were uncertain times with uncertain outcomes. The only way to tackle this was through planning and accountability. For that, people would need to step up and extreme ownership would be a must from all. So before starting to plan or write out a strategy that needed to be executed, I sent an email to all my forty direct reports.

The email stated, 'Dear esteemed colleagues, the ongoing COVID-19 pandemic has brought a sharp surge in the number of complaints from our cherished customers. We have experienced sudden unavailability of staff and significant delays in customer waiting times across all customer-facing channels. We recognize that our staff and customers are equally frustrated with our current situation. As a result, we are organizing a virtual full-day offsite meeting to plan how to get things under control and improve our performance to meet and exceed customer expectations. The meeting is scheduled to take place within a month, providing ample time for each of you, being veterans in your respective fields, to prepare. This is a unique opportunity for all of you to come up with one project that will be your brainchild, and you will be solely responsible for ensuring its delivery from start to finish. The theme of your project should be happiness and how to make this organization one of the most joyful environments for employees and customers. Meeting invites shall be sent shortly. Best regards, AZ.'

Sure enough, one month later, my personal assistant had received forty project plans. The plans were so good that we had to increase the offsite from one day to three, eventually selecting twenty-one plans. Out of the twenty-one projects, the team delivered eighteen. Some of them were unable to be delivered due to dependencies on system upgrades. Although all the staff were fully busy and even though we were hit with a pandemic, they did the extra work with a smile and full of energy. Why? Because they were involved in the planning and strategy from the beginning. It was their brainchild, their baby.

Having plans is not enough. For full ownership, the plan needs to be tracked and reported on periodically. Below, I have listed the actual outcomes within twelve months of starting twenty-one babies.

Year end Performance (NPS/CSAT score missing)

Product	Target	Jan	Dec	Comments
CSAT	85%	15%	81%	Major improvement in CSAT
Service Level (SLA)	80% in 30 seconds	15%	81%	Major improvement in Service levels
Quality Assurance (QA)	90%	54%	90%	Major improvement in Quality
Turnaround Time (TAT)	1 Day	3 Days	8 Hours	Major improvement in TAT
NPS	55	28	46	Major improvement in NPS
Service Time	10 Minutes	31 Minutes	7 Minutes	Major improvement in Service Time
Productivity	95%	72%	97%	Major improvement in Productivity
Waiting Time	20 Minutes	97 Minutes	16 Minutes	Major improvement in Waiting Time

The steps involved in delivering such stellar outcomes:

1. Involve all managers in your team at the time of planning.
2. Send them an email with the problem you are trying to solve and give them ample time to come back to you.
3. Specify that it is one project per individual with each person having full accountability to deliver the idea that has been selected.
4. Add the selected ideas and projects to individual KPIs.
5. Hold monthly meetings with the team to track progress.

As you climb the corporate ladder and your team grows in size, success will come to you only if the team gels and each person takes on responsibilities they can excel at while perfectly executing the plans. Since they will be executing their own plans, they will be passionate about them and want to see them fulfilled, instead of feeling the disconnect caused by a top-down approach where we see corporates giving us targets and objectives without us knowing why they are important or how the targets were set.

Tip: To successfully deliver your organization's strategy, it is critical to consider your organization's ability to execute. Hence, the importance of identifying and utilizing your team's strengths in areas that matter and can deliver optimal results.

This involves breaking down the overall plan into smaller specific tasks that can be carried out by the right people. As a leader, it is your responsibility to establish a culture and processes that promote efficient execution.

This includes identifying and rewarding individuals who demonstrate a strong track record of getting things done quickly. To effectively execute, it's important to set clear priorities based on your understanding of the business. In fact, embedding execution into a rewards system will further incentivize individuals and teams to stay on track.

Tip: Consistent follow-up is key to ensuring that tasks are completed as planned.

CHAPTER HIGHLIGHTS

Empowerment through ownership: Involve your team in the planning process from the very beginning and see them take ownership of their projects. When individual members feel a personal connection to the plan, they look forward to its success and go the extra mile with gratitude.

Foster collaboration and communication: Ensure that communication and collaboration within your team are promoted. Monthly or quarterly coaching sessions help. This will significantly boost alignment and ensure that everyone's efforts are on track.

Reward performance: It is important to recognize and endorse strong performers for their dedication and stellar achievements. This will help build trust and motivate others, helping them excel in their respective roles.

Team contributions: Nothing can make a team member feel more valued than involving them in the decision-making process. Show them that their input is essential for your team and the overall success of the organization.

Utilize subject matter experts: The involvement of individuals who will be executing the plan and are the subject matter experts is critical while you are still in the planning phase. Their insights and expertise will lead to more realistic and effective plans and, at the same time, will ensure their full buy-in.

Create a culture of accountability: Lead by example and demonstrate a strong commitment to accountability. Motivate the team to take on more ownership by recognizing individual contributions. Hold regular progress meetings to assess the plan's implementation and address any challenges while not forgetting to celebrate the individuals who have supported the team's growth.

Continuous learning and fair evaluation: A culture of learning and development will provide opportunities for skill-building and knowledge-sharing, fostering personal growth and improved performance backed by a fair and transparent performance evaluation system that recognizes and rewards high performers and addresses performance issues through constructive feedback and coaching.

Tracking team progress: Keeping track of your plan's progress and adapting when necessary to your ever-evolving and changing circumstances will cement a culture that will cause talent to gravitate towards your style of leadership, creating a pool of talent to cherry-pick from.

Collaboration: Promote collaboration and teamwork within the organization. When team members work together and support each other, they become more productive as collaboration is key to faster results.

Create a culture of ownership and accountability and lead yourself and your team to greater success in executing your plans and achieving superior results for your organization and customers. Remember, planning and ownership go hand in hand, and when executed effectively, they become the driving forces for success.

CHAPTER 15
LEADING ONE'S BOSS

Quantity Versus Quality And
Managing Upwards

While working hard, we forget to work smart. One way to work smart is to measure our work in terms of the value it delivers instead of the workload or quantity delivered. The simplest way to do this is to break it down in the following format:

Tasks vs Value

1 – No Impact | 2 – No Impact (Must Have) | 3 – Low Impact | 4 – Medium/High Impact | 5 – Very High Impact

#	Task	Value	Remarks	Tracking
1	Staff Training	2	Delegate	Quarterly
2	Seating alignment	1	Delegate / Eliminate	Not Required
3	Government Integration Mandate	5	Critical / Own	Weekly
4	Process Online Journey (Digital migration)	4	Focus / working group	Bi-Weekly
5	Real time KPI Report development	4	Focus / working group	Bi-Weekly
6	Manager / Staff rotation	3	Delegate	Monthly
7	Dashboard redesign / revamp	2	Delegate	Quarterly
8	Extra TV In meeting room	1	Delegate / Eliminate	Not Required
9	Knowledge Base Review	3	Delegate	Monthly
10	Document archive arrangement	1	Delegate / Eliminate	Not Required

Each of the above tasks may take the same amount of resources, energy, and time to deliver. However, one or two of these tasks will add five to ten times the value of any of the others. When you have too many tasks, the one that usually gets the least of your attention is the task that, if completed, will deliver the highest return. Why? Because it will be the most difficult, so we tend to leave it till last and focus on the tasks that are more numerous and may take the same time but are easier to deliver.

In this case, a leader craftsman thinks and keeps aside the easy, low-value tasks and delegates them, if needed, or removes them altogether and focuses on the big catch, which will deliver the most value if completed.

THE 80/20 PRINCIPLE

The 80/20 principle was discovered in 1897 by Italian economist Vilfredo Pareto. The study proved that not every activity or task delivers an equal payoff, and that the right few selected efforts deliver most of the output and results.

You are not trying to be busy. That is not your key to success. Your key is to be productive. For that, first, you need to figure out what actually matters and what will have the biggest impact. Focus on the 20% that has the biggest impact. Do not add anything new until that task is completed.

80/20 Rule

The 80/20 rule suggests that 80% of the outcomes come from 20% of the inputs or efforts, highlighting the concept of prioritizing the most impactful actions for maximum results.

By identifying and focusing on the most impactfully activities we can achieve more while doing less.

Fig A

effort / results / 20% / 80%

20% efforts on activities that would give 80% overall results

While quality versus quantity in tasks, projects, and activities is important, we should, at the same time, take quality versus quantity into consideration when looking at our teams. We need to make sure we have the right team in place with the right skill set and size. A larger team does not mean you will have better results. Work, as mentioned earlier, is not defined by quantity. Work is defined by results. Having a huge number of staff under you might make it look like you rule an empire, but if you do not have the right people and a proper system in place to identify your team gaps, how to bridge those gaps, the proper tools, resources, and development needed, and how to flush out the rotten apples from the system, you will be overwhelmed by the issues and problems this large team brings to work and creates through their everyday interactions.

MANAGING YOUR BOSS

As a leader, you must not only be able to manage downwards, but you have to manage your stakeholders, and your biggest stakeholder is your boss. Managing upwards is key for any leader to be successful. As a leader, you must be able not only to lead your followers but you must have the skills to manage upwards, which can be a great challenge for leaders as they often are inspired to lead without being led themselves. However, remember that all bosses value having others add value to them.

By taking an approach of adding value to those above you, while doing your work with excellence, you have started to distinguish yourself from the rest. Constantly adding value in this way can help your leader to learn to trust and rely on you, potentially making you their go-to person and having you on their speed dial when they need support. The undertaking of such a strategy of adding value and supporting one's superior must be approached with caution, as it is critical that one does not approach the task in a manner that overshadows the boss. As emphasized in Robert Greene's book *The 48 Laws of Power*, never outshine the master.

Do not become credit-hungry as you will be given tasks that are bigger than your role. This is not the time to show off with your boss' boss and boast. It is the time to learn and become your boss' right-hand man. Credit will come in due time and through the right channel.

You will get many opportunities to bypass your boss. However, never do this. Always keep them in the loop and ensure they are the first to know if an issue arises. Even if you get a task from another superior, always let your boss know. You never put them in a situation where you have discussed something with others that they are not aware of.

Become the individual who always delivers the work that you have agreed to do and on time without ever being reminded or chased by your boss. Build your reputation as a person who gets things done. Supply only accurate information. If you do not know the answer, make it a practice to say, 'Let me make a note of that, find out, and get back to you.' And make sure to always get back as committed, and within the timeframe that you set.

Checking information is better than assuming and giving wrong information. Accurate information builds credibility. Assumptions gone wrong destroy credibility. Rather than pretending to know the answers to every question, it is better to confess a lack of knowledge and then follow through by seeking out accurate information. This demonstrates integrity and reliability, and it will establish a credible reputation and make you a valuable asset to your boss and the organization.

I remember a time when I was given a golden opportunity. The chairman of the organization in which I was working at that time called me to get something done urgently. I passed it on to my subordinate because I had some other work that I was busy trying to complete. It was a small task, a phone call that needed to be placed to a customer. My subordinate, who called the customer late, was unable to close the issue at hand and forgot to notify me. Guess what happened next? The customer called the chairman and complained for the second time. The chairman called me in turn and asked me what went wrong. I had no idea since I was not the person who made the call. I told the chairman, 'Let me call you back after asking my subordinate.'

The chairman was disappointed and told me, 'Ahmed, if I wanted someone else to handle this customer, I would have called them. Anyway, thank you for providing such excellent service to our customers.'

Can you guess what happened after that?

THE CHAIRMAN NEVER CALLED ME AGAIN!

The moral of the story is to know what is important and what is urgent, and opportunities will come. Build your bridges with all stakeholders, but make sure, in the process, to never burn your bridge with your own boss.

Tip: How well you build your reputation with your boss, or let's call it creating easy access, depends on how prepared you are when you attend meetings with your boss and other stakeholders. Effective and meticulous preparation is an essential ingredient for triumph in any field, whether it is a high-stakes executive board meeting, delivering a speech, or giving a presentation.

When you show up to a meeting fully prepared, you project a can-do attitude and a hands-on vibe that cannot be detected in the mediocre manager. Not only will you leave the meeting feeling more confident, but everyone present will hold a more positive opinion of you, and this will boost your overall reputation.

In summary, effectively managing upwards requires creating an environment in which your boss can depend on you for support and accurate information by providing support that adds value to your boss and the organization. Rather than solely focusing on your individual performance, focus with honesty and attention to detail, which portrays reliable behavior. In doing so, you increase your value and influence with your boss and with the organization.

One technique to manage upwards effectively is through reverse coaching, where the responsibility to get coached on a monthly basis lies with you, not your boss. Everyone wants to be better; everyone wants more.

Everyone is hungry for credit and development, yet no one seeks or takes action. Your job is to time-block one hour a month of your boss' time so you can give them a detailed update on everything you are doing and ask for guidance regarding your performance. Are you meeting expectations? What can you do better? What should you stop and what should you start doing? Make sure all is documented and closed before your next meeting.

I had a boss who was a very successful CEO and extremely busy. We met one day, and he told me I was doing a great job, but he was not satisfied with my performance. He expected ten times more from me. Now, I had never heard that before. It was the first time. However, what are your thoughts on this? Is it my boss' fault for having such high expectations of me or my fault for not delivering? Well, the answer is neither. The problem was not having clear communication, which, as a master craftsman, was my responsibility to ensure was occurring and that there was documentation for me to review to make sure I was on track and delivering as per my boss' expectations.

CHAPTER HIGHLIGHTS

Strive for value: Emphasize the importance of measuring your work in terms of the value it delivers rather than the sheer quantity. Prioritize tasks based on their impact and focus on those that bring the most significant returns.

80/20 principle: Apply the Pareto principle to identify the 20% of efforts that yield 80% of the results. You will be concentrating on high-impact activities and will be avoiding the unnecessary hustle and bustle.

Managing upwards: Understand the significance of building your relationship with your boss. Support them by adding value, delivering outcomes with excellence, and being reliable in your commitments. Have regular clear communication with your boss, updating them on your progress, while seeking guidance and understanding their expectations to ensure you are aligning your efforts with their vision.

Reverse coaching: Make it your duty to seek feedback from your boss regularly. Request guidance on your performance, areas for improvement, and ways to better meet their expectations.

Preparation, preparation, preparation: Show up on time fully prepared, demonstrating a can-do attitude and a sharp attention to detail. Effective preparation is a natural booster of confidence and always leaves a positive impression on people you come into contact with.

By focusing on the above points, you will be enhancing not only your leadership skills but your ability to manage upwards effectively as well. Overall, you will build a strong, positive reputation within your organization and among your stakeholders and peers. Remember, the key is to think in terms of value while maintaining open communication and striving for continuous improvement.

AUTHOR BIO

Unlock the insights of a seasoned visionary and industry luminary with more than two decades of transformative experience. Meet Ahmed Al Zarooni, a trailblazer who has journeyed through diverse sectors, leaving an indelible mark on the realms of leadership.

Ahmed's narrative is one of mastery and innovation, honed through deep-rooted expertise in building exceptional leaders to drive operational efficiency. His prowess extends to the realms of environment and mindset transformation, change management, multi-channel optimization, risk management, and the pursuit of cultural excellence.

A beacon of operational brilliance, Ahmed Al Zarooni has pioneered a culture of excellence, placing a premium on both the development of future leaders and unparalleled customer experiences. His journey has been shaped by a relentless pursuit of enhancing both industry landscapes and the lives of those they touch.

Not only does Ahmed bring a treasure trove of practical wisdom, but his academic laurels shine just as brightly. His accolades include a coveted Fintech Certification from Harvard, a Leadership Certification from the prestigious Oxford Said Business School, and a Masters in Business Administration from the esteemed University of Wolverhampton.

Ahmed's influence doesn't stop at achievements. He has seamlessly transitioned into roles of governance, serving on the boards of numerous distinguished institutions. His contributions as a board member and supervisory board member have not only enriched his own journey but have also catalyzed transformation across organizations.

Prepare to embark on a journey through the corridors of wisdom and innovation, guided by Ahmed Al Zarooni's unique insights and pioneering spirit. Join him as he unravels the secrets of building leaders, harnessing the power of strategic planning, and orchestrating environmental metamorphoses. Through the pages of *A Leader's Legacy*, Ahmed invites you to witness the convergence of experience, academia, and vision – a trifecta that has shaped his remarkable odyssey.

Connect with Ahmed Al Zarooni on a voyage of inspiration, where his words become a compass to navigate the ever-evolving tides of leadership and excellence.

NOTES AND REFERENCES

CHAPTER 2. Mastering Leadership

Brain size: Yuval Noah Harari, *Sapiens: A Brief History of Humankind*, HarperCollins Publishers, 2015.

CHAPTER 3. Leadership Overview

His Highness Sheikh Zayed bin Sultan Al Nahyan quote: *Father Of Our Nation: Collected quotes of Sheikh Zayed bin Sultan Al Nahyan*, Motivate Publishing, 2017.

The word 'leadership': *Oxford English Dictionary.*

Leaders are eager to learn and don't fear making mistakes: Warren Bennis, *On Becoming a Leader*, Basic Books, a member of the Perseus Books Group, New York, Printing 21, 2021.

CHAPTER 4. Becoming Responsible

Increase our own value by working harder on ourselves: Jim Rohn, *The Five Major Pieces To The Life Puzzle: A Guide To Personal Success*, Embassy Books, 2011.
BlackBerry case study: https://business.time.com/2013/09/24/the-fatal-mistake-that-doomed-blackberry/

Average baby falls 38 times a day: https://www.veipd.org/earlyintervention/2014/01/09/toddlers-weeble-wobble-and-fall-down-when-is-it-cause-for-concern/

CHAPTER 5. Anchors And Ladders

His Highness Sheikh Mohammed bin Zayed Al Nahyan quote: https://stepfeed.com/7-wise-quotes-that-define-sheikh-mohammed-bin-zayed-s-leadership-4555

6,200 thoughts a day: http://bigthink.com/neuropsych/how-many-thoughts-per-day/

Square-shaped watermelons: www.japanesefoodguide.com/square-watermelons-japan/

Codie Sanchez, YouTube channel, experiment: https://youtube.com/shorts/-uBZvahKs?feature=share

NOTES AND REFERENCES

Reference group: Darren Hardy, *The Compound Effect: Jumpstart Your Income, Your Life, Your Success*, Hachette Book Group, Inc., 2020.

In your search for excellence: Robin Sharma, *The 5AM Club, Own Your Morning Elevate Your Life*, Thornson's: An Imprint Of HarperCollins Publishers, 2018.

CHAPTER 6. Goals And Planning

Greek mythology: www.britannica.com/topic/sisyphus

Darren Hardy quote: Darren Hardy, *The Compound Effect*.

Only about 3% of adults: Brian Tracy, *Eat That Frog, 21 Great Ways To Stop Procrastinating And Get More Done In Less Time*, Berrett-Koehler Publishers, Inc., 2017.

CHAPTER 7. Mastering Your Craft

Jim Rohn quote: Jim Rohn, *My Philosophy For Successful Living*, No Dream Too Big Publishing, 2011-2012.

Keller Papasan writes: Keller Papasan, *The One Thing: The Surprisingly Simple Truth Behind Extraordinary Results*, Rellek Publishing Partners, Ltd., 2012.

Earl Nightingale quote: Earl Nightingale, *Your Greatest Asset: Creative Vision & Empowered Communication*, Nightingale Conant Corporation, 2019.

Brian Tracy statement: Brian Tracy, *Million Dollar Habits: Proven Power Practices To Double And Triple Your Income*, Entrepreneur Press, Publisher, 2017.

Self-development through feedback: Marshall Goldsmith, *What Got You Here Won't Get You There: How Successful People Become Even More Successful*, Profile Books Ltd., 2013.

CHAPTER 8. Time Check Priorities By Time-Blocking

Prioritizing tasks: Mikael Krogerus & Roman Tschappeler, *The Decision Book: Fifty Models For Strategic Thinking*, Profile Books, 2011.

Most important tasks: Josh Kaufman, *The Personal MBA: A World Class Business Education In A Single Volume*, Penguin Books Ltd., 2010, 2012.

Self-reflections: Earl Nightingale, *Lead The Field*, BN Publishing, 2006.

Cal Newport's research: Cal Newport, *Deep Work: Rules For Focused Success In A Distracted World*, Piatkus An Imprint of Little, Brown Book Group, a Hachette UK Company, 2016.

Multitasking exercise: Jeff Sutherland & J.J. Sutherland, *Scrum: The Art Of Doing Twice The Work In Half The Time*, Currency, An Imprint of The Crown Publishing Group, 2014.

Stop doing the wrong things: Nir Eyal with Julie Li, *Indistractable: How to Control Your Attention And Choose Your Life*, Bloomsbury Publishing, 2020.

CHAPTER 9. Culture

The word 'culture': *Oxford English Dictionary.*

Daniel Coyle writes: Daniel Coyle, *The Culture Code: The Secrets of Highly Successful Groups*, Bantam Books, 2018.

Research conducted at The Harvard Business School by James Heskett and John Kotter: www.growthengineering.co.uk/corporate-culture-and-performance-whats-the-link/

HBR, 71% of senior executives: https://www.booqed.com/blog/minutes-wasted-of-meeting-50-shocking-meeting-statistics

https://truelist.co/blog/meeting-statistics/

Meetings described by Peter F. Drucker: Peter F. Drucker, *The Effective Executive: The Definitive Guide to Getting the Right Things Done*, HarperCollins Publishers, 1967, 1985, 1996, 2002, 2006.

CHAPTER 10. Rings Of Influence

Simon Sinek writes: Simon Sinek, *Leaders Eat Last: Why Some Teams Pull Together and Others Don't*, Portfolio/Penguin, 2017.

Jim Collins writes: Jim Collins: *Good To Great: Why Some Companies Make The Leap And Others Don't*, Harper Business, 2001.

CHAPTER 11. Mastering Team Strengths

Peter F. Drucker quote: Peter F. Drucker, *Managing Oneself*, Harvard Business School Publishing Corporation, 2008.

John C. Maxwell, in his book: John C. Maxwell, *The 5 Levels of Leadership: Proven Steps to Maximize Your Potential*, Center Street, Hachette Book Group, 2013.

CHAPTER 12. Environment

Larry Bossidy asserts: Larry Bossidy & Ram Charan with Charles Burck, *Execution: The Discipline of Getting Things Done*, Currency an Imprint of The Crown Publishing Group, 2009.

NOTES AND REFERENCES

CHAPTER 13. Enhancing Connections

His Highness Sheikh Mohammed bin Rashid Al Maktoum quote: *Quotes: Mohamed bin Rashid Al Maktoum, Life,* Motivate Publishing, 2022.

The rise and fall of Eastman Kodak: www.ajhssr.com/wp-content/uploads/2020/12/ZB20412219224.pdf

Trust means confidence: Stephen M. R. Covey with Rebecca R. Merrill, *The Speed of Trust: The one Thing That Changes Everything,* Free Press An Imprint of Simon & Schuster, Inc., 2018.

CHAPTER 15. Leading One's Boss

The 80/20 principle: Richard Koch, *The 80/20 Principle: The Secret of Achieving More with Less,* Nicholas Brealey Publishing, 2017.

Never outshine the master: Robert Greene, *The 48 Laws of Power,* Viking Press, 1998.

Notes

Milton Keynes UK
Ingram Content Group UK Ltd.
UKHW021920190224
438095UK00006BA/279